Viewing

A BBC producer's memoir of changing times

Viewing History

A BBC producer's memoir of changing times

Keith Bowers

© Keith Bowers, 2013

Published by Pavenham Press

A CIP catalogue record for this book is available from the British Library.

ISBN 978-0-9575011-0-2 (paperback)
ISBN 978-0-9575011-2-6 (epub)
ISBN 978-0-9575011-1-9 (mobi)

Cover design by Clare Brayshaw

Cover Image © Press Association

Prepared and printed by:

York Publishing Services Ltd
64 Hallfield Road
Layerthorpe
York YO31 7ZQ

Tel: 01904 431213

Website: www.yps-publishing.co.uk

Dedication

To my daughter Bridget who provided the inspiration
and the encouragement

Contents

About the Author

Keith Bowers is a highly experienced television producer and programme editor, who had a twenty year career at the BBC. He was the deputy editor of the flagship BBC programme, Newsnight, and he launched the award-winning international documentary show, Correspondent. At one time he was the executive in charge of all BBC international current affairs programmes on radio and television. Since leaving the BBC he has coached many aspiring film-makers and journalists in many corners of the world. In all, he has worked in more than 40 countries and loves exploring places undergoing rapid and dramatic change.

Acknowledgements

I didn't view history on my own: television is team work. There isn't space to mention all the many colleagues and friends from around the world who have shared my adventures. Many are named in the course of the book and I am deeply grateful for their help.

Television journalism is not for the faint-hearted and can be a tough, competitive business. However, I have received generous support from many reporters, producers, camera crews, editors and fixers. In recent years, I have also loved working with many students across the world, helping to prepare them for the exciting and challenging world of journalism. I would like to highlight those whom I deeply respect or who have given me extra support. Some truly special people fall into both categories.

From the start of my career, I would like to thank Chris Anderson, now the curator of TED. I worked with him on a radio station in the Seychelles and he greatly encouraged me to go to see India for myself as a fledgling journalist.

At the BBC Newsnight programme, I am especially grateful to two of the programme's editors, John Morrison and Tim Gardam, who sent me on a number of fabulous assignments. It was a great team, but I especially enjoyed working with David Sells, Steve Anderson, Amanda

Farnsworth, Bridget Kendall, Eileen Fitt, Jeremy Bristow, Irene Ozga, and Jon Barton.

I have also worked with some great journalists who sadly are now dead – Charles Wheeler, Nick Clarke, Ian Smith, Brian Hanrahan and the producer Helen Jenkins, who watched my back when I had my first executive producer's job at Assignment and Correspondent.

The team at Assignment and Correspondent was fantastic, but special thanks must go to Fiona Stourton and Julian Pettifer, and to my impressive colleague in radio, Maria Balinska. Mark Damazer was also a great boss as head of current affairs.

In my post BBC career, I have to thank the team at Gimlekollen Media College in southern Norway who sent me on many training assignments to the Balkans and Ethiopia. My old friend, Knut Sigurd Aasebø, made it all possible, and I loved working with Kåre Melhus, Jon Ragne Bolstad and Kenneth Andresen. Øyvind Aadland passed on to me his passion for Ethiopia and for the Amharic language.

In Kosovo, Avni Ahmetaj and Florent Gorqaj provided good-humoured support and kept me going.

In Ethiopia, there are countless people who have helped me in so many ways. They include local workers such as Abel Adamu, Yemane Tsegaye, Henok Mebratu, and Adanech Admassu. Kaylois Henry and Ragnhild Ek are among international friends and colleagues I want to thank.

I am deeply grateful to those who have read part or all of my manuscript and given me invaluable feedback – John Owen, Carola Frentzen, Tracy Pallant, Ewa Ewart,

Yidnekachew Shumete, Solomon Hailemariam, and Helen Buhaenko. Peter Snow also passed on some helpful comments as well as writing a preface. However, as always, any mistakes in the book are down to me as the author.

Many of the photos in the book were taken by me. A special thanks to my team mates who took the others, especially Carola and Yidnekachew while on location at a Mursi village in Ethiopia.

The staff at York Publishing Services helped to guide me expertly through the complexities of getting a book published. Special thanks to Cathi Poole, Paula Charles to Stephanie Milson who did the proof reading and to Clare Brayshaw for the layout and cover design.

Preface

This is a wonderfully exciting and absorbing read. Keith Bowers' career has been a set of worldwide adventures that few journalists experience in a lifetime. He has already held almost every documentary post of interest in the BBC and is now a highly creative independent producer.

Some of these adventures, as you will read, we shared together. My favourite memory is the same one as his. We witnessed the collapse of the Soviet empire in 1989 and 1990. It wasn't just the end of the iron grip the Kremlin held on Eastern Europe. It was the collapse of Communism as well, and of the Cold War that for my generation was the paramount issue in world affairs. Quite suddenly the whole flawed system crumbled. And the author of this book was there, and he tells the story with all the enthusiasm and flair that I remember so well when we worked together. Keith reminds me, and television viewers who watched the programme he produced that night, of the extraordinary moment when the very first rubble from the demolition of the Berlin Wall was set down on a table before me in an East Berlin studio.

Moments like that, and Gorbachev's struggle to manage change in Russia, the Israeli election that brought Rabin to power and opened the way to a deal with the Palestinians, and the unravelling of Thatcher's premiership in Britain – all these were stories that made history. Keith was there and gives us a heart-stopping taste of the tension and sometimes confusion of editing a live TV programme.

But this book is about a much wider field. It includes Keith's other daring escapades in investigative journalism. He witnesses the last days of apartheid in South Africa. He is sent on a perilous mission to rescue a BBC team under arrest in Yemen. He pursues illegal gold-diggers in Brazil, secrets of the demilitarized zone between the two Koreas, and dangers and opportunities in the Balkans and Ethiopia.

Keith Bowers is a skilled documentary film-maker, and his accounts of the way he carried out his wide variety of challenging missions are compelling enough. But he is also a very perceptive observer and writer, whose descriptions of the great statesmen and women he meets are superbly crafted, witty, and revealing. *Viewing History* is aptly named. It is an enthralling read and a great testament to the achievements of its author.

Peter Snow

Introduction

One day in 1981 while living in the Seychelles, I found myself sitting engrossed in thought on the gorgeous Beau Vallon beach on the main island of Mahé. Normally on my days off from working on a radio station on the island, I would be happy just to relax, to soak up the sun and swim in the warm waters of the Indian Ocean. But this day was different. I was feverishly thinking ahead to the following day when I would have an opportunity to cover the visit to Seychelles of the then Indian Prime Minister, Mrs Indira Gandhi. I was only 26 at the time and she was going to be by far the most influential figure I had ever had the chance to meet in my fledgling journalistic career.

Indira Gandhi had already been at the vortex of incredible historical change. As the daughter of Pandit Nehru, India's first prime minister after independence in 1947, she had witnessed the horrors of partition when hundreds of thousands of Hindus and Muslims were slaughtered during the massive displacement of people from both communities. She went on to become India's first female prime minister and had come under fierce international and domestic criticism for her imposition of a state of emergency in the mid-seventies. Mrs Gandhi was already on her fourth term in office by the time she was due to visit the Seychelles.

I was not disappointed when I saw Mrs Gandhi at a press conference at the end of her trip to the islands. She certainly came across as an imposing, larger-than-life character. There was no formal opportunity to ask her questions from the floor, but afterwards we journalists were allowed to mingle informally with Mrs Gandhi and the socialist leader of the Seychelles, President France-Albert René. I almost disgraced myself when I nearly tripped over the feet of the President, who at that stage was something of a hard-liner with a reputation for cracking down on political dissent. Suddenly I found myself face to face with Mrs Gandhi. Although somewhat nervous, I managed to have a brief informal conversation with her about the Seychelles, which she described as being like a big beautiful garden.

This encounter gave me the impetus to pursue a journalistic career with more intensity. I now knew I wanted to have a front row seat at significant current events and scrutinise major opinion-formers first hand. After returning to the UK from the Seychelles, I was lucky in early 1983 to get a job as a scriptwriter in the BBC television newsroom. It was a perfect time to be on the market, as the BBC was starting breakfast television and therefore had some rare vacancies in its news division.

I spent about eight months in the BBC newsroom before being transferred to the Newsnight programme, the BBC's flagship daily news and current affairs show. For the first few years, I was mainly studio-bound as a desk producer. Nevertheless, I still had the chance to feel close to unfolding political events through booking leading politicians and opinion-formers for interviews. However, I still harboured the desire to be out and about in the thick of the journalistic action, especially abroad.

Soon I had earned my spurs and was being sent out of the office as a field producer. One of my first foreign trips was to produce *Newsnight*'s coverage from the film festival in Cannes in 1987, a dream assignment. I had not tasted such glamour since living in the Seychelles. I was the producer for the *Newsnight* presenter Joan Bakewell, who had shot to fame in the sixties as the intelligent presenter of the ground-breaking *Late Night Line-Up* show.

During our stay we interviewed the imperious actor Alec Guinness on a yacht moored off the spectacular Promenade de la Croisette. While we were editing the Guinness interview at our base in the British Pavilion in Cannes, we had a visit from Prince Charles and Princess Diana. They were guests at the festival and were keen to see some creative activity. We tried to keep our cool as the Prince came into the editing suite ahead of his wife. He saw Alec Guinness on our screen and proceeded to talk at length about his prowess as an actor, especially his role in the *Great Expectations* feature film. The Princess said nothing and kept herself in the background. Suddenly, the editor began to rewind the video tape, with the rapidly reversing sound track giving off a loud noise: beep, beep, beep, beep.

Quick as a flash, the Princess piped up: "Oh, it sounds just like me."

I was impressed and amused to see her adopt such a self-deprecating stance. As we know, in later life, she was to prove herself no shrinking violet, and became an agent of change in her own style.

So first Mrs Gandhi, then Princess Diana; two very contrasting famous figures who both made their mark on history. However, my building fascination with the shifting sands of current affairs went way beyond an interest in iconic personalities. As a producer on *Newsnight*, I was caught up in many of the great ideological shifts sweeping through the world in the latter stages of the twentieth century – the decline of communist power in the Soviet Union and Eastern Europe, the continued bitter wrangling over the future of Israel and Palestine, the growing struggle against apartheid in South Africa, and the rise of powerful Asian economies, including Japan and China. As the former British Prime Minister Harold Macmillan is reputed to have said, it was all about "events, dear boy, events."

This book focuses on some of those epoch-making events I have witnessed as a television producer over the last 25 years. It homes in on some of the key pressure points and fault-lines of the modern age. Some of the changes involve dramatic transitions of political and territorial power in which ideological tectonic plates have shifted with tremendous force. Others involve environmental changes, such as the degradation of the Amazonian rain forest, and the social and economic transformation currently sweeping through African countries.

The book describes encounters with a wide variety of people, ranging from the famous to the humble to the eccentric. Looking back over my career, the unifying theme has been that of covering change. It is what makes the world – and our lives – intriguing and engaging.

Viewing History adopts an observational and informal approach, backed up by anecdotes and eye witness accounts. It does not attempt to provide all-embracing, detailed analysis of the events outlined. Instead, the book concentrates on describing a number of specific historical and contemporary snapshots, seen from my perspective as a television producer on the ground. It is designed to give a sense of what it was actually like to be there and to meet some of the extraordinary characters caught up in those events. The book is therefore not a traditional memoir; it is much more about being an observer of the events themselves rather than a vehicle to explore my own life and beliefs.

The style of *Viewing History* is akin to that of *From Our Own Correspondent* on BBC radio. I have always admired the programme and indeed, for a number of years at the BBC, I had some managerial and editorial responsibility for *FOOC*, as it is known. At the time, I was the Executive Editor in charge of all international current affairs output on BBC radio and television. I have always championed an observational style in reporting, believing it is vital to get out of the office and see for oneself what is actually happening on the ground. Although I left the BBC in 2002, I continued to explore different parts of the world as a freelance producer, and teacher of aspiring journalists and programme-makers in places such as the Balkans and Ethiopia. *Viewing History* covers key events dating back to the late eighties, but also has material from right up to the present day. The world keeps on changing.

Some of the material in the book is based on diaries written at the time or on notes compiled shortly after the various events. Hopefully, this provides a fresh and raw perspective, and gives different insights into some events, such as the fall of the Berlin Wall, which may be familiar.

This book is not just an account of some of the tempestuous changes in recent times; it also reveals the daunting editorial and logistical challenges faced by television producers as they wrestle to broadcast their stories on location against the clock. I hope these accounts of how television works behind the scenes will provide some revealing and entertaining insights.

I am conscious that some of the events covered in this book occurred in a different time, before the explosion of the internet and digital technology. When I first started working at the BBC around thirty years ago, there were few mobile phones to speak of. I remember being given one of the earlier models when producing an item from the Albert Hall about the Westland Helicopters crisis in the mid-eighties, which nearly brought down the Thatcher government. The new-fangled phone was totally impractical as the signal kept cutting out and it was incredibly heavy and clunky, like carrying an ugly brick with a bulbous antenna.

Office computers, like the internet, were also in their infancy. Most people thought that chips were something you ate out of a paper bag. I recall having to dictate the intros I had written for the BBC's main news bulletins to secretaries, who bashed out the scripts on typewriters and provided copies on carbon paper. The technological changes we have all experienced in the last 25 years have been truly revolutionary and match some of the other transformations mentioned in this book.

The broadcast media landscape has also greatly altered during my professional lifetime. At the beginning of 1983, there was no *Sky News*, no *BBC News 24* or *Al Jazeera*. CNN had been on the air for less than three years. The VHS machine had not long been on the scene, and electronic newsgathering was slowly coming into its own.

Political and cultural attitudes were also vastly different during the early eighties. Thatcherism was in full swing and so too was the Cold War, with the reforming Gorbachev still some time away from making his spectacular entrance onto the world stage. Saddam Hussein was a close Western ally, not a dreaded enemy, and coal mining was still a major industry in Britain. The terrible events of 9/11 in the United States, causing the western world to obsess for long periods afterwards about perceived and real terrorist threats, were still some way off.

CHAPTER ONE

Berlin – Climbing The Wall

Along with many millions of other people, I refused to believe it. When first told of the rumour that the Berlin Wall was suddenly going to be opened, I simply shrugged my shoulders and carried on with what I was doing. On the night in question – 9 November 1989 – I was in the bowels of Television Centre in Shepherd's Bush, viewing a routine film which was going to be shown on *Newsnight* later that evening. Although I was in overall charge of the show that night, I saw no reason to be distracted. Despite the optimism of the summer of 1989, with refugees from Eastern Europe pouring across the borders of Hungary and Czechoslovakia, the story of the collapse of the Wall was too much to believe. After all, that infamous structure had been gruesome evidence of the division between East and West since my childhood. Its unwholesome reputation had been reinforced through a string of spy movies and cheap novels.

I had long had a fascination with this forbidding symbol of repression, but had not seen it with my own eyes until the autumn of 1988. I was in Berlin during the making of a two-part series on the challenges posed to the West by the then Soviet leader, Mikhail Gorbachev. My colleague on the project was Peter Snow, the energetic and authoritative *Newsnight* presenter, who enthused madly on camera under the lee of the Wall, "There are even some dreamers who believe that one day this Wall could be breached, setting off a new era in East-West relations."

After recording this piece to camera, we chuckled knowingly to one another; the Wall to us looked as if it had claimed a permanent pitch in Berlin, and we had no sense that the dreamers would have their day any time soon.

Such memories conditioned my insouciant response when told of the rumours that the East German authorities had effectively opened up the Wall on that seemingly routine day in November 1989. However, all that changed when there was a second urgent phone call to the Television Centre editing suite where I was lurking. The early reports had been true: history was indeed being made that night. By this stage, it was around 7.30pm. We hurriedly scrapped all our plans for that evening's *Newsnight* and cobbled together a relevant programme with a completely new running order.

We could not do justice to such a momentous event, of course, and after we came off air we gathered in my office to draw breath. We had to decide how we were going to cover this gigantic story the following day. Naturally, along with every other television outfit across the world, we wanted to present the programme from Berlin – but did we have the right staff with the right experience available? Several of our senior producers were off-base on other projects so, to my great surprise and delight, the spotlight turned on me, now normally desk-bound as the programme's deputy editor. The editor of *Newsnight* at the time, John Morrison, asked if I would go to Berlin. I obviously jumped at the chance. Who wouldn't want to be present at such a decisive turning point in history?

I rose early the next morning to catch the first plane from Heathrow to Berlin. The flight was packed with camera crews, producers and reporters – all full of anticipation and nervous energy. My travelling companion was again Peter Snow and we had another rueful chuckle to one other about his piece to camera only a year before. On arriving in Berlin, we wasted no time. We dived into a taxi and set off for the Wall, just by the Brandenburg Gate, where we had recorded Peter's now prophetic comments twelve months previously.

What an awe-inspiring sight greeted us: there were thousands of exuberant revellers massing on the streets, many of them climbing on top of the Wall, previously a banned and dangerous activity. The section by the Brandenburg gate was quite high, about eight feet or so. I found it difficult to scramble up, especially with the heaving throng dancing wildly and recklessly above. Still, I managed to get there with a bit of help. However, Peter was struggling to make any progress until a posse of well-wishers shoved him from below. At the same time, I managed to grab his arms and pull him to the top. Later, Peter told me it was that feeble attempt to climb the Wall that made him realise that age was beginning to creep up on him.

When we had got our breath back, we surveyed the historic scene around us. On the other side of the Wall, down below, were the hated East German border guards. They were completely bewildered; up until now they and their ilk had harried and shot any transgressor who had dared step on the Wall and threaten the sanctity of the East German communist state. They had never witnessed such a spectacle and were clearly at a loss as to what to do next. Nobody had any orders to give. Fear of the unknown was clearly etched in their eyes.

The West Berliners were relishing the discomfiture of the East German guards, though many other emotions were being expressed by those standing astride the two previously unbridgeable worlds. People everywhere were euphoric and amazed at being at the centre of such a poignant turning point in history.

It was hard to be a detached journalistic observer. This was a privileged ringside seat at the denouement of one of the biggest ideological straitjackets of the twentieth century.

Eventually, Peter and I reluctantly realised that we would have to say farewell to this eruption of carefree joy. We somehow had to retrieve our detached professionalism to put out a live programme that night in very chaotic circumstances. First, we had to cross over to East Berlin, where our studio facilities had been booked. As tension had mounted ahead of the Wall coming down, BBC News had been operating from a base in East Berlin and transmitting pictures from the state broadcasting headquarters there. It was, perhaps, a sign that the East German regime had

4

already started to open up, but it may also have been that the authorities were desperate to make some money by hiring out their facilities.

The first challenge was to get across Checkpoint Charlie, one of the most famous crossing points. To get there, we first walked by the Wall for a few hundred metres; it was like being part of a heaving, excitable Wembley cup final crowd. Most of the area was wasteland but there was the occasional tree dotted here and there. One foolhardy acolyte of democracy had climbed into the flimsy branches of one of these trees to try to gain a grandstand view of proceedings. He seemed oblivious to the danger as he swayed alarmingly up above the mass of gesticulating and incredulous people. He seemed like a symbol of how a free spirit can conquer all.

We reluctantly left this area to pick up a hire car and then drive to Checkpoint Charlie. Again, everywhere was packed with ecstatic crowds. Hundreds of people were pouring across from East Berlin. Many of them were stepping foot in the West for the first time. As each new batch of these pilgrims made it to West Berlin soil, car hooters sounded in a frenzy. People leaning out of windows in elevated office blocks cheered and applauded. We were in a slow-moving queue to enter East Berlin but we were not bored. We were absorbed in listening to the breathless, excitable announcers on Armed Forces Radio, who were revelling in describing the historical events all over the city.

At the border itself, there were more confused East German officials struggling to keep any remnants of the discipline that had ruled their collective psyche for the last

28 years. They were simply overwhelmed by the crowds, and people were allowed through without much fuss.

The scene on the East Berlin side was a great contrast. There were no delirious crowds massing near the Wall; it was a much more uncertain atmosphere, more of a repressed hysteria. East Berliners were not finding it easy to suddenly throw off their chains. People were still wary of the guards and approached them gingerly. The surroundings also bore witness to the failures of the East German regime. The roads were in a dreadful condition. Many of them were being dug up, creating an untidy sprawl. The office buildings were drab and uninviting, and the standard of vehicles on the road was terrible. The ubiquitous Trabant car, which was made out of cheap, flimsy materials, was no match for the well-heeled Mercedes and Audis which graced the elegant thoroughfares of West Berlin.

Our initial destination was an exception to this dreariness and told something of a different story. We headed for the opulent Grand Hotel, which had been built in a joint venture with international capital. The hotel was a show case as only foreigners paying large amounts of hard currency could stay there. It was an example of the social divide in East Germany between the elite and the masses.

The Grand was modern, lavish and imposing. What's more, it worked. The efficient phone system and professional customer service seemed totally out of place in a run-down socialist city on its last legs. Being there was yet another bizarre experience on this memorable day. The bedrooms were grouped around an impressive atrium, with the ground floor bedecked with large pot plants, grand pianos and swish, gleaming bars.

We hunted for the *Newsnight* film team – which had already been in East Germany for several days – and eventually found them five floors up. Both the reporter, Olenka Frenkiel, and producer, Jon Barton, were exhausted. They had experienced even more than we had. They had been among the first to storm onto the Wall in the hours of darkness the night before, and had recorded a vivid piece to camera surrounded by crowds waving sparklers. During their earlier travels round East Germany, they had sensed the impending collapse of the state's authority. They were in tremendous spirits. We agreed that in the upcoming *Newsnight* programme that night they would tell in a recorded video package how the momentous day had unfolded. Peter's and my job was to worry about how to pull off a successful introduction to the show, and to find some guests to take part in a live discussion.

While we quickly discussed our plans, room service was summoned. Within minutes, a tray of high-class sandwiches had arrived. On the platter were finger rolls decorated with fresh smoked salmon, egg mayonnaise and cress, and thin slices of delicious soft cheese. Could this really be East Germany? It seemed East had met West in the Grand hotel kitchen way before the demolition of the Wall.

Around us, other television crews were scattering hither and thither, trying to meet deadlines for live interview spots and news flashes. I was accosted by one BBC sound recordist who seemed impervious to the fact he was in the middle of a political earthquake. All he wanted to know was whether I had any spare East German marks. Apparently there was a great killing to be made on the black market. I found it hard to believe that this was his preoccupation at such a momentous historical juncture, though I supposed it showed that capitalism was flourishing in the East.

In the middle of all this chaos, I managed to get a call through to our office in London. They had found a guest in West Germany who was prepared to try to travel to East Berlin to take part in a live discussion. His name was Thomas Kielinger, the chief editor of the *Rheinischer Merkur* newspaper, based in Bonn, West Germany. He could not guarantee getting to our studio in East Berlin, and we weren't that optimistic either. Up until the previous night, he would have had no chance of crossing over without arranging special permission in advance.

I remained confident that we would be able to transmit something from East Berlin, but was achingly aware that we still had to overcome many imponderables. One of these was finding the studio, which was hidden away in a nondescript part of town. I decided to tag along with a producer from the *Six O'Clock News* when he went to feed his video material to London. It was quite a depressing journey through run-down streets before ending up on a massive industrial site. The television building was a testimony to the soulless vision of a communist state. It had been built on a huge scale, presumably in the fifties, and had long, uninspiring corridors and decaying plasterwork. I fully expected to see the East German equivalent of Lord Reith stalking round the place.

There were technicians everywhere, but it was not clear who was in charge. Somehow the material for the *Six*

O'Clock News was relayed to London. However, there were already ominous signs that pressure was mounting on the circuits out of the country, as the rest of Europe and the world woke up to the full implications of the tumbling of the Wall. I managed to get a look at the studio allocated for our use. It was a great barn of a place with no redeeming features. The only thing to shoot against was a plain background and there was a set of furniture which looked as if it had been bought at a Sunday morning car boot sale. The East German director was quite a sight and did not fill me with much confidence. He was a tall man in his forties, with longish hair and a scrawny, grey beard. I could not help but ask myself what such an ageing Woodstock hippy was doing in such a barren place, seemingly devoid of any artistic spark.

Back at the Grand Hotel, the normal frenzied activity before encroaching deadlines manifested itself in groups of people running round the corridors overlooking the atrium. The editing of our material was going slowly, and I realised that our satellite booking later that evening was not going to be long enough both to send over a recorded video package and then switch to the live discussion. The only choice was to feed some unedited pictures earlier on the feed for the *Nine O'Clock News*, and for the *Newsnight* team in London to stitch the material together there.

Peter and I then rushed off to record the vision links which would introduce the *Newsnight* programme. We decided to do these against the backdrop of Checkpoint Charlie. There was still a reasonable queue of people desperate for their first taste of life in the West, so we were hoping it would make an effective opening shot. However, when we watched the shot back on the monitor it appeared a little flat. Perhaps it was just that it was impossible to convey the intense atmosphere through a camera lens.

Normally we would have expected unwelcome interference from fussy communist officials while filming but tonight, amid the general chaos, there was mercifully none. However, it was becoming clear that the earlier euphoria had dissipated somewhat and that the guards were becoming a little more officious. The top of the Wall by this time had also been cleared of dancers and some semblance of normality was returning.

Afterwards, I had to rush back to the Grand Hotel to pick up the first part of Olenka Frenkiel's report. This was already running into problems and we were in great danger of missing the first feed back to London, the disaster scenario. In the end, I simply had to snatch the tape and set off in a dash for the television station. I paused only to issue instructions to Olenka and Jon to try to get some pictures of the Wall being knocked down – an operation which was rumoured to begin later that night, around the time we were on air.

As usual, the clock was against us, though I was very glad I had done the dry run to the studio earlier. It was a much-experienced nightmare, roaming at great speed through foreign streets, straining to meet a satellite deadline. In my earlier career, I had once run into a glass revolving door at a television studio in Dublin while rushing in with a tape. It was quite painful but even more embarrassment was to follow. Still feeling disorientated and woozy from the collision, I almost bumped into the then Irish Prime Minister Dr Garret FitzGerald, who was standing in a corridor waiting to go on air.

I think it was a good job the Berlin authorities were preoccupied with far more important issues on this historic night, otherwise I am sure we would have been hauled up for speeding. We certainly cut it fine and just managed to send the material right at the end of the feed.

All should now have been well; the second half of the Olenka piece would easily fit onto the second booked transmission feed and there was also the prospect of some new dramatic pictures of the Wall being demolished. Despite much seemingly aimless scurrying around, the studio preparations were under control. The hippy director was staying cool – but things can change quickly when live television is involved. There was soon a tremendous problem establishing a live sound link with London and there was also no sign of Thomas Kielinger. I was not surprised about his non-appearance, given the remote location of the studio and the chaotic nature of the day.

Fortunately, our other main guest, Jens Reich, had turned up. He was one of the leaders of the New Forum movement, which had been pressing for more democracy in East Germany. This was a big boost for the programme as he was an articulate spokesman for the forces of change, and had become something of a familiar figure in the West.

With just a few minutes to go to transmission, I went outside to scour the deserted streets for Thomas Kielinger. I remained pessimistic but, much to my astonishment, I discovered him at one of the security entrances to the television station. He was even more surprised to see me and could not believe he had made it to East Berlin. He had been mildly rebuked at the border for not having the correct visa papers, but the guard had realised that there was no point in stopping him. He only gave Kielinger a bit of a telling off, after learning that Kielinger was trying to go to East Berlin to take part in a BBC programme.

"Why don't you speak to East German television instead?" the guard admonished. Like just about everyone else that day – apart from the black market bargain-hunting sound recordist – Herr Kielinger's face was a mixture of confusion, incredulity and excitement about being in Berlin at this time. On air later, he described the experience as mind-boggling and said he felt he had been reborn.

In the end, all was going smoothly with the transmission of the programme. The sound problem had been solved and all the VT material had been despatched to London. The ageing hippy and his technical team were working well and the discussion was lively enough. The only disappointment I had mid-way through was that there was no sign of Olenka and Jon with any new pictures of the Wall being demolished.

However, they suddenly turned up while the discussion with Peter Snow, Jens Reich and Thomas Kielinger was in full flow. Jon's face was straining to control his exuberance.

"No pictures, Keith, I'm afraid," he said jauntily, "but look at what I've got."

At this point, he brandished a dusty brick which they had snaffled when the authorities had bull-dozed a section of the Wall to make an extra official crossing point. I am sorry to say my first reaction was a bit negative. "All very interesting but what use was that?" was the first thought that ran through my mind. I was fixated on getting pictures – it was television, after all. But both he and Olenka were determined to ensure their prize had full exposure and they suggested that Olenka interrupt Peter Snow and march on set with the brick itself.

They were absolutely right: what a great idea. There followed a debate as to whether we needed to mike Olenka up and indeed whether such an unexpected intervention could be handled by the East German crew. We also had very basic talkback facilities with Peter. Despite the confusion, Olenka was able to approach Peter with the brick, and somehow managed to get his attention and place it on the studio table.

The response to the brick being plonked down in front of Kielinger and Reich provided what was regarded as one of the best television moments of the coverage of the crumbling of the Wall. Kielinger enthused about the German spirit, and the spirit of freedom and enterprise. Jens Reich, tears in his eyes, uttered with marked understatement: "Marvellous. I would never have dreamed to have seen a brick from the Wall. It is fine."

We were understandably euphoric after the broadcast, though we knew how close the whole enterprise had come to disaster. I was also glad that we had managed not only to capture some of the amazing twists and turns of an historic day but had also raised some important questions of substance. Could the authorities ever re-impose restrictions on crossing the border? How many of the East Germans who had flocked to visit the West would return? Would the East German government deliver on its promises of free, secret and democratic elections? And then the big question – would there ever be a united Germany? Jens Reich thought that was still a long way off, but of course he turned out to be wrong, as within a year or so Germany became one.

However, Reich did give a memorable warning, putting the celebrations in perspective. He said he would be unwilling to give up some of the social principles of the East because he was wary of the West, where everyone seemed to have opted for what he called an 'elbow' society.

Peter and I were not booked in at the Grand Hotel in East Berlin, so after a welcome drink at one of the thriving bars there and a hurried discussion about what to do over the weekend to prepare for Monday's programme, we headed back to our hotel in the West. By this time, Checkpoint Charlie had calmed down, but we went to bed knowing there would surely be more excitement to be had on the next day.

The weekend in a rejuvenated Berlin was a happy-go-lucky affair. Altogether around a million and a half people from the East were estimated to have crossed into the West on the Saturday and Sunday. The streets were full of animated crowds attracted by novelty, curiosity and a sense of daring. They were like schoolchildren lapsing into indiscipline and silliness when their teacher is called away from the classroom.

It was a time of high emotion. I spent much of Saturday morning in heated discussion with one of our teams sent out from London as reinforcements to help cover the unfolding events. I also made another trip over to the Grand Hotel back in the East. This proved to be very time-consuming, as the hordes simply overwhelmed the officials at the crossing points. I went there to try to talk to Olenka, as it was not yet possible to phone directly from the West to the East. We had tried to communicate via our team in London but even this overworked circuit had disappeared. In the event, my trip proved to be fruitless; Olenka and her team had left very early for Dresden and all I could do was to leave a note for when they returned.

I had a tortuous journey back to the West, though again the atmosphere was intoxicating and exhilarating. It was a shame I couldn't just relax and enjoy everything without having to worry about producing what I knew would have to be a big and impressive programme on the Monday night. I was aware that, by then, many other programmes would have had a bite of the story, so we had to come up with something fresh and different. Peter Snow had dashed back to London for the weekend to attend a couple of personal engagements, so I was left alone with my own thoughts – but not for long.

I heard from London that even more reinforcements were being sent and I had to sort out some hotel rooms for them. It was madness. Half the word's media plus entrepreneurs and opportunists were on their way. After spending the day spinning like a top, I was happy to spend a convivial evening at a little café called Einstein, hoping it would provide the required intellectual inspiration for Monday's show.

It was the same frenzied story on the Sunday, which dawned grey and cold. By this stage, the area in front of the Brandenburg Gate was under siege from a welter of satellite dishes, OB vans, and camera platforms. A cacophony of anguished production voices in a variety of languages mingled in the air with the continued gleeful chatter of Berliners.

While the two *Newsnight* filming teams beavered away on either side of the Wall, I became bogged down in a series of complicated meetings with engineers and technicians. The BBC machine had suddenly been turned up to maximum warp speed. We now had been asked to plan an ambitious programme live from inside the old Reichstag parliament building. Panorama also wanted to stage a discussion there just before our show, so everything was very invigorating.

By Monday, even the top brass of *BBC News* and *Current Affairs* had arrived. The overall boss Tony Hall and newsgathering chief Chris Cramer were desperate – like everyone else – to witness history at first hand. Presumably, they were also keen to see how a gargantuan portion of their budget was being spent. I had to break off from preparing the programme to explain to them what we were up to. There were also dozens of logistical arrangements to juggle. One of the most difficult problems was keeping track of all the people who were now working for *Newsnight*; the production staff alone had now swelled to around twenty.

We also had two programme guests: the former Tory Prime Minister Ted Heath and the former Labour Defence Secretary Denis Healey had been booked by the London team. They had both agreed to fly to Berlin to take part in the *Newsnight* show from the Reichstag. I imagined that this was a rare occasion when these two political warriors did not curse under their breath when called by *Newsnight*, who usually wanted them to defend some tendentious policy issue.

The countdown to the programme was a blur. We had to keep the Reichstag officials happy, find a major West German guest, wrestle with an octopus-like running order, and keep in touch with our teams scattered around Berlin and beyond. In addition to these arrangements, there were constant phone calls with London to liaise on vital matters of technical circuitry, timings and editorial direction. It was nothing like the pandemonium inside the governments of East and West Germany, but it was nonetheless enough for a headache the size of the Brandenburg Gate.

Despite everything, I thought things were broadly under control until about an hour before transmission. Olenka's East German team had gone missing and I began to fear that they would not be able to cross over to us and deliver the tape of their edited story. Much worse, there was no sign of Edward Heath. A story began to filter through about his plane being late or being diverted elsewhere.

There were no such problems for the larger than life Denis Healey, who had already arrived, full of bonhomie and enthusiasm. He was whisked off to the Wall by one of our producers and was filmed merrily practising his German on a hapless border guard. Eventually, his old adversary Ted Heath arrived, looking somewhat angry and aloof. He didn't bother to shake anyone by the hand, unlike Denis Healey, who could not refrain from constantly clapping people on the back and tweaking his infamous bushy eyebrows. There was just enough time to film the rather withdrawn Heath toasting the crowd around the Reichstag before we had to concentrate on the final countdown in the makeshift studio.

With just a few minutes to go to transmission, we realised that Ted Heath had disappeared once again. Maybe his alcoholic celebrations had already caught up with him, but for whatever reason, he had made a bee-line to a toilet hidden away down a winding corridor. The Reichstag may have been a building which resonated with history, but it was infuriatingly good at concealing important guests! I had to despatch a posse of producers to find him. To his eternal credit, Peter Horrocks, who had been in charge of the earlier *Panorama* inject from Berlin, was able to discover the bathroom where Mr Heath had hidden himself away. Peter, who later was to become Director of *BBC World Service*, showed his mettle by calling out in a polite but firm voice that could Mr Heath please hurry. Mr Heath in the end arrived on set just in time.

The irrepressible Denis Healey could not allow himself to be upstaged in this way. Just ten seconds before Peter Snow read the live introduction to the show, Denis the joker produced a plastic eye from his pocket and proceeded to attach it to his own face. The object dangled bizarrely on a piece of wire, though if Peter Snow was amused by this spectacle he managed not to show it. Denis Healy was already well-known in the trade for such antics. I once heard how he had tried to ruffle the poise of Peter Sissons, then a presenter on *Channel Four News*, by giving him 'v' signs underneath the desk if he did not like a question he was asked during a live interview.

The two battle-hardened guests, Heath and Healy, certainly delivered on air, despite their vastly different warm-up routines. Healy described Berlin as the happiest city he had ever been in; Heath pointed out how most East Germans were prepared to give their government one last chance by returning to East Berlin, despite sampling the attractions of the West. There were no problems at all with the content, which did the occasion proud, but there were a few technical gremlins. At one stage, I had to run full-pelt from inside the Reichstag to the OB van parked outside after a panic-ridden call from London complaining about sound quality. There were also problems with some of the camera angles and the vision mixing. Under the circumstances, with an almighty traffic jam on the world's technical circuits, I felt it was a creditable achievement.

I was especially pleased with the sense of history that the programme had managed to convey. We had two original reports from both sides of the Wall. Olenka began her piece with pictures of a concert in the opera house in Dresden given by the rock singer Veronika Fischer, dubbed East Germany's Madonna. Fischer had not been back to East Germany since she had escaped across the Wall ten years earlier. In the best traditions of *Newsnight*'s party pooping tendencies, Olenka warned of political uncertainties to come. She also raised the spectre of what was to become a very divisive and unpleasant social problem – what to do with the hated Stasi, who had terrorised the population with its vicious surveillance methods.

In his report from West Berlin, Julian O'Halloran also pointed out some dangers ahead. Even though only six thousand or so East Germans had expressed a wish to stay permanently in the West, the West Berlin authorities were not able to cope. Finding housing and jobs would become a nightmare and there were more accurate predictions of the chaos that could ensue when many more disillusioned East Germans demanded a slice of the capitalist action. His report also dwelt on the thorny issue of reunification, which Chancellor Kohl had raised in what turned out to be a widely unpopular speech in Berlin at the weekend. O'Halloran concluded by lamenting that Kohl seemed to be pushing the economic and political philosophy of the West down the East's throats.

The live discussion was not as prophetic as the two VT reports. Healey dismissed Kohl's comments as stupid demagoguery which was out of touch. Ted Heath was asked if the democratic fever would spread to the rest of Eastern Europe; he mused that he could not see President Caescescu of Romania catching it very fast – that the opposite was more likely. However, less than two months later, Caescescu was to be deposed and killed in a deadly revolution in Romania.

We had escaped without serious mishap. It had been a very challenging programme to get on the air and, as the credits rolled, I was ready to take a break from the twin pressures of witnessing history and producing live television. "What about some German beer and nourishment?" someone shouted, so off we went round the city looking for a local hostelry. Sadly, the city seemed exhausted by the convulsions of the last few days and we could not find any restaurant open to feed us. We did eventually find a place to down copious amounts of beer, but I was just too shattered to really appreciate it.

It was nearly all over, bar the filling in of expense forms. The spotlight was moving away from Berlin to the rest of Germany and how the historical changes would affect the Soviet Union and its relations with America.

Given all that, no piece was therefore required for the next day, so most of us were able to draw breath and go off sightseeing – or, to be more precise, to go on a rock hunt. By this stage, countless hordes had begun chipping away at the Wall for souvenirs. Ted Heath, true to his understated performance throughout, cleared off early, but the exuberant Healey, still clutching his phoney eye, joined us for a trip over to the East. We thought the pickings from the Wall there would be better, as the East Berliners were likely to be more circumspect in attacking the line of concrete which had subjugated them for a generation.

There were huge queues to cross back into East Berlin, but Denis kept us entertained with a stream of scatological jokes about the former American president Lyndon Johnson and other luminaries he had encountered during his barnstorming public life. How ironic to be part of a group of bounty-hunting sightseers with a former British Defence Secretary, whose task once had been to ensure that the East Germans were kept in line.

As we meandered along the now-defunct border, we came across a section of wall that was virtually untouched. The guards in evidence here seemed to have recaptured

On a tour of the Wall with Denis Healey. I am on the right of him with Mark Gregory, a Newsnight producer, on the left

some of their previously mean demeanour. However, buoyed by Healey's good spirits and sense of adventure, we managed to pick surreptitiously at the odd lump. It was surprising to see the poor handiwork of those who had built it. Once you made a small hole, it often crumbled into tiny, flaky bits. We were only able to extract one or two viable pieces and I doubted whether this shoddy rubble would survive the journey home by the time we landed at Heathrow.

Fortunately, one of the reasonably large fragments I had mined did arrive in one piece, though later I had to jealously guard it from my destructive small children. Humans under four – especially those with no concept of the Iron Curtain or spies – were not worried about smashing priceless artefacts of history. My colleagues back at the *Newsnight* office were rather more impressed with pieces of masonry from the Wall when I eventually turned up there, somewhat dishevelled, later that night. It all seemed like an amazing dream. As for the brick which brought tears to the eyes of Jens Reich, I think that was raffled off for Children in Need.

BERLIN REVISTED

On the tenth anniversary of the fall of the Wall in 1999, I was able to fly back to Berlin. I went back with the distinguished journalist and historian Timothy Garton Ash, with whom I was working on a special series. All the memories of 1989 resurfaced. Then, we had had a chaotic entrance into the cramped airport; this time it was different. The organisers of a Freedom Forum conference we were attending were anxious to ensure that Tim arrived in time to speak at a special dinner at the Reichstag. We were whisked through passport control and set off at break-neck speed. It was a thrill to see the Reichstag again, with its new spectacular glass dome, designed by the British architect Norman Foster to commemorate the unification of Germany.

My hotel was in the newly built Potsdamer Platz. In 1989, it had been a drab open space; now it was full of shimmering steel and glass skyscrapers. I much preferred this new East Berlin. It had now recovered its elegant past round Gendarmenmarkt, and well-designed hotels and shops had sprung up. Even Café Einstein, one of the best features of the old West Berlin, had got in on the act by opening a new modish café on the Unter den Linden in East Berlin.

On the Monday, there was another highlight; I was one of the specially invited 200 guests to the Axel Springer building to see a discussion involving three influential figures of history – President George Bush senior, President Gorbachev and Chancellor Kohl. Timothy Garton Ash was the moderator. Gorbachev was rambling but at the end he did say something intriguing. He believed that, in some ways, things had gone backwards since 1989, a somewhat sobering judgment contrasting with the backslapping self-congratulations of Bush and Kohl.

There was also an amusing moment when Bush was asked about the ten-point plan for German unity put forward after the Wall fell. He declined to comment, saying he couldn't even remember what he had had for lunch two days ago. By then he was 75. All this in a week in which his son, George W., then a presidential hopeful, had been humiliated because he did not know the names of the leaders of India, Chechnya and Pakistan – like father, like son. Afterwards, we were swept along into a posh buffet where the three protagonists jostled with the rest of us for their prawns and curried chicken. Gorbachev, who looked downcast just weeks after the death of his beloved wife, Raisa, was accompanied by his granddaughter.

It wasn't all work, of course. One producer, Fred Baker, took me to watch the rugby World Cup final in an East Berlin bar, where chanting French and Aussie spectators had a great time winding each other up. We also went to the hippyish alternative venue, Tacheles, to hear an amazing bout of Russian music, which transformed every type of melody under the sun from Doris Day to 1920s rag. Berlin never fails to disappoint.

AN ENCOUNTER WITH TWO ANTI-COMMUNIST HEROES

I had the chance to meet Vaclav Havel in 1999, during the filming of a three part series on Eastern Europe fronted by Timothy Garton Ash. I tagged along as the show's executive producer. We interviewed Havel at the Magic Lantern theatre in Prague, the nerve centre of the Czech Revolution ten years before. He had been a prominent playwright who had suffered for his beliefs and had been a worthy agent of change by leading the so-called Velvet Revolution in 1989.

Havel took us on a tour of the theatre and we went into the projector room, where he watched old footage of himself as a conspirator. In those revolutionary times he was a raffish figure, wearing an open-necked shirt and looking relaxed – a contrast to his presidential appearance ten years on, wearing a smart dark suit and tie. He now moved stiffly and looked ill at ease having to live the life of a formal statesman. When Havel ran the underground headquarters of the Czech opposition, he and his fellow activists knew that all the phones were bugged. To counter this, so the story goes, they had an extension line installed from a flower shop above, where the phone sat on a washing machine.

During our filming, Havel really struggled for breath while climbing some stairs and I was terrified he was going to keel over. I could just see the Daily Mail headline: "Heartless BBC team kill courageous intellectual."

While making the Garton Ash series, I also had the opportunity of meeting another firebrand opponent of East European communism, Lech Walesa. He was the fiery shipyard worker from Gdansk who was instrumental in establishing the Solidarity trade union movement.

I went with Tim to the gates of the of the Gdansk shipyard where Walesa had plied his trade. On camera, Tim described Walesa then as being skinny, small and feisty, not the grand, portly statesman he had since become after a stint as president of Poland.

As Walesa showed Tim around his office in town, I filmed the scene for a trailer for the series. By this stage, Walesa was no longer a national hero and had been heavily criticised for what were seen as his dictatorial tendencies while he had been president. Walesa told us that he believed Poland had suffered a moral decline after the end of communism; he was also hard on himself, saying, "I have a kind of moral hangover. We should have done more for the workers."

It was sad to see such a physical and ideological decline in a previously heroic figure. What had happened to that erstwhile revolutionary? It was such a contrast from meeting Havel, who, despite problems with ageing, had still kept the revolutionary flame alive.

After meeting Walesa, we filmed in one of the abandoned warehouses of the Gdansk shipyard. The children of the strikers' generation were dancing to heavy techno music and viewing a weird fashion show staged by a Ukrainian designer. Male and female models with grey painted circles on their faces carried candles while dressed in shrouds. The strikers of the eighties regarded such activities in their shipyard as blasphemy. However, it was clear that the world had moved on and Walesa and his former colleagues had not come to terms with it.

CHAPTER TWO

Russia – Goodbye to Lenin

I was nervous about making my first trip to Moscow at the end of February in 1990, even though I was being given the chance to lead a large *Newsnight* team to cover a key period in Mikhail Gorbachev's rule of the Soviet Union. It was not that I feared being the victim of the building unrest against the communist system; indeed, I was enthused by the outside possibility that my working visit there could turn out to be another Berlin experience, though I realised that witnessing another such poignant and far-reaching moment of historical change was being unrealistically greedy. Neither was I worried about the difficulties of producing live television in a city where the economy was breaking down and a black market was flourishing. In fact, I was looking forward to the challenge of not operating by the rules for a change.

No, my nerves were jangling mainly due to the prospect of experiencing at first hand the harsh Russian winter. After all it had done for Napoleon and Hitler, what chance had a cosseted inhabitant of BBC Television Centre? I had already been destabilised by a story told by one hardy BBC correspondent about going for a pee outside in the

Russian winter; he had had the disconcerting experience of watching his urine freeze before his disbelieving gaze. I had also not settled back into coping with even the relatively feeble British winters after living for two years in the tropical sun of the Seychelles – so what chance would I have in February in the city of the Kremlin, with its famed sub-zero temperatures?

I knew that making television programmes in such Arctic conditions would not be easy. With so little daylight and extreme cold, it would be difficult to film anything outside and rushing around to meet the satellite deadlines would also be problematic. Call me soft, but I had a healthy, gnawing fear of Russia's General Winter.

In the end, I need not have bothered getting so worked up; on arrival in Moscow Airport, the temperature was exactly the same as it had been in London. In the fading afternoon light, I was driven in a battered taxi to the centre of the city. The driver was in a foul mood and said: "Just look at this winter. Why, even the Moscow River isn't frozen. What's happening to this country?" His insecurity was understandable – not just because Muscovites have a penchant for skating on the river when it is thirty degrees below but because he, like many others, was nervous about anything out of the ordinary, especially at such a time of political and economic turmoil. Now even the ice had melted unexpectedly and this was taken by the taxi driver as a portent of doom. For me, of course, it was a huge relief. If caught short in the open air, I could pee without getting frostbite and any dash to a satellite feed point would be much more straightforward. I took the mild weather as an omen of success for the trip.

Of course, leaving aside my rather neurotic fears about the rigours of a Moscow winter, I was delighted to be there. Of all the places I felt I had to visit to further my journalistic education, the Soviet Union was top of my list.

There was also no doubt that the winter of 1990 was a fascinating time to be in Moscow. Gorbachev was very popular in the West for his arms control concessions and apparent commitment to glasnost (openness) and perestroika (restructuring of economic and political systems), but it was becoming clear that he was regarded increasingly without honour at home. Indeed, I was surprised to discover the contempt he was held in by many ordinary Russians we met. Gorbachev was becoming the butt of many jokes fashioned by the famous black Russian sense of humour. For instance: "What's the difference between a misfortune and a tragedy?" Answer: "A misfortune is when Gorbachev goes for a walk on the walls of the Kremlin and falls off. A tragedy is when he goes for a walk on the walls of the Kremlin and returns unscathed."

One of the great purveyors of Russian humour was our chief driver, Vitaly, an invaluable member of our production team. He was a great bear of a man, in his late twenties and constantly decked out in a black leather jacket. Unlike most inhabitants of the creaking Soviet empire, Vitaly was blooming. His gifts of wit and likeable cunning were great assets in a growing black market culture. He had been recommended by a BBC producer from a previous visit, and Vitaly was smart enough to see that good old Auntie was a rich source of dollars. In fact, he could hardly believe his luck. This *Newsnight* project in Moscow was big business for him.

The trip had been commissioned by the incoming *Newsnight* editor, Tim Gardam. He wanted to make his mark quickly, so no expense was to be spared. He put me in charge of a massive team; three reporters, four producers, two camera crews, two picture editors, a translator, a director and a PA. With hired local help, the team stretched to twenty at one stage during the three week trip. I would never see its like again in television and Vitaly was one of the beneficiaries of one of the last gasps of big budget current affairs coverage.

When I first met Vitaly his eyes had gleamed when I told him of our requirements. We needed transport at any time of day or night and worked out that up to five cars would be required. For a wheeler dealer like Vitaly that was no problem, and he said he could easily rustle up another four adventurous chancers like him. Our deal was concluded late in the evening while standing in Red Square; he had taken me there to see the sights. I was certainly impressed with the scale and beauty of the nearby Kremlin, with the hammer and sickle flag lit up and billowing in an artificial jet stream. The onion shaped domes of St Basil's Cathedral also provided an incongruous aesthetic backdrop to my grubby deal-making with Vitaly.

It could have been the stuff of a Hollywood film – two men whispering animatedly in the centre of Red Square with a few flecks of wet snow swirling in the night air. But, instead of dealing in political intrigue, we were simply embracing the new entrepreneurial spirit seeping into the psyche of Muscovites. In the end, we settled on five US dollars a day per car. Vitaly wanted no contract or any other paperwork to present to the tax authorities unused to such capitalist activity. My only problem was working out how I would account for this bizarre deal on my expenses form when back in England.

Vitaly was a constant source of stories and inside information about this new 'wild east'. He was utterly cynical about the political process and resigned to the economy collapsing further. However, he never let us down and showed remarkable resilience and ingenuity to meet the needs of a voracious television road show. One of his finest achievements was in procuring some tickets for the Bolshoi ballet when we had a Saturday night free. One of the items on the programme was Petrushka, Stravinsky's baleful tale about a love-sick puppet. The standard of music and dancing was tremendously high – as you would have expected. What really made it an unforgettable occasion was the exquisite Bolshoi theatre, with its ornate tiers of seating and maroon fittings. It was as if Lenin, Stalin, Khruschev and Brezhnev had never existed; it was quite easy to imagine sitting there in the same row as Tolstoy, with the splendours of the Tsar's court in full swing. The experience was one of many contradictions I was to experience during this visit. I saw quite a lot of subtle beauty in a generally drab city with many examples of hideous communist architecture, especially the ubiquitous dreary blocks of apartments.

This visit to the Bolshoi came towards the end of a hectic few days of filming, editing and live programming. The main idea of our visit was to cover some important local elections in the Soviet Union, one of the country's first attempts at democracy. We had planned to produce discussion programmes from a makeshift studio, with Peter Snow as anchorman. To complement this, we would run a series of film reports by the elegant Francine Stock, who had spent a couple of weeks in the unstable Baltic states, and the redoubtable Charles Wheeler, who had turned his steely eye on the rebellious state of Georgia. All this endeavour was taking place of course before the Soviet Union split asunder, and some of our reports hinted that the great empire was in its death throes.

The first piece in our season of programmes was produced by me and reported by Peter Snow. Hardly anyone else had arrived by the day of transmission, so I was forced into doing what I loved: going out on the road and filming. Then there was the ultimate job satisfaction

Just to prove I was there. On the banks of the Moscow River with the Kremlin in the background.

of sitting down with a picture editor and working out how to put the piece together. The item had a simple aim – to explore Mikhail Gorbachev's precarious position as party general secretary.

We decided to structure the piece around three people: a radical lawyer called Oleg Lyamin, who thought Gorbachev had not gone far enough in his reforms; a soft spoken yet determined old-style communist academic, Alexi Shulus, who felt Gorbachev had betrayed the revolution and the Soviet people; and an ordinary worker, who just happened to be called Mikhail and, like the country's leader, also had a wife called Raisa. Perhaps not surprisingly with such names, the couple supported Gorbachev, but – maybe a little like the general secretary himself – they were confused and unsure about which way to take the country.

The short film was punctuated with some dramatic and unexpected events. Our first meeting with the radical campaigner Oleg was at the defence ministry, where he had organised a demonstration for the mothers of soldiers who had died while in army service. He had evidence that they had been bullied to death by cruel superior officers but the authorities were insisting that the soldiers had committed suicide. Before meeting Oleg, I had assumed that the protest would be a relatively tame affair. After all, this was happening in the cradle of communist Russia, where open dissent had a habit of leading to the unwelcome attentions of the KGB or other security services.

However, when we arrived, a determined band of formidable Russian women was storming up the steps outside the defence ministry. They were demanding an interview with someone in charge. Perhaps the sight of a Western camera crew gave the mothers extra courage, because they then pushed open the door and swarmed into a dingy corridor inside. Here they set on bemused guards, who were impotent in the face of this formidable assault by women waving photos of their dead sons. One guard demanded that one woman show her passport. She brandished a photo of her dead son in his face and shouted, "That's my passport!" before storming past him.

We duly followed the mothers and were amazed to see such an open flouting of authority. We were even more surprised that we were not prevented from filming this outburst of democracy in action. Eventually, the angry mothers were ushered out with the promise of a meeting with a senior officer. After a while, this encounter was held in a room in the shadow of a portrait of Lenin, who no doubt would have been perturbed to have seen such disrespect for the Soviet system. The women were livid and scented blood. The senior official was forced to make some concessions and it was a clear victory for the underdog. I was dumbfounded; things like this were not supposed to happen in the land of the infamous and brutal Lubyanka Prison. For me, it was a clear sign that the teetering communist regime would not have long to run.

Oleg too was incredibly angry about the bullying by Red Army officers. He told us the story of one Russian army cook who refused to give food to some pigs kept by his commanding officer. The cook said the men were hungry and it was they who needed the food. However, the callous officer simply had him killed for his disobedience. We also witnessed raw displays of emotion when we attended a meeting of the hard-line United Workers Front, supported by Alexi Shulus, who was critical of Gorbachev for, in his view, moving too far away from the communist system. Shulus was on the official platform but he could only watch helplessly as the audience tore into each other in a bitter wrangle over what tactics to adopt in the forthcoming elections. This was another sign that passions were running high and the previously stable communist edifice was in danger of tumbling down.

Our suburban couple, Mikhail and Raisa, were not caught up directly in such passionate political disputes, but they were subjected like everyone else to the desperate daily struggle for a passable existence. We went shopping with Raisa to a local shop which was virtually empty. Despite this, she was quite pleased with even the limited range of goods on offer. There was no red meat and sugar was rationed, but she was delighted to see some chicken on the shelves.

The manageress, loyal to the communist system, buttonholed our crew and began eulogising about the triumphs of the command economy. She even boasted that there had been live fish for sale the day before. She was cut down wonderfully by an elderly female customer who was within earshot. She interjected and said there was nothing in the shop and it was a complete disgrace. We could not resist filming later at the new branch of McDonalds, which had struck a blow for capitalism by obtaining permission to open in Moscow. Here there was plenty of meat on offer and, perhaps as a result, the queue snaked back in the street for a few hundred metres.

We stayed at the Cosmos Hotel, one of the few places where journalists could operate from. It was a huge aircraft hangar of a building and was situated opposite the so-called Park of Achievement, where the miracles of Soviet Communism are celebrated. From my window high on the seventh floor, I could see a phallic structure commemorating Soviet exploits in space.

Despite the proximity of the Cosmos to this haven of Soviet achievement, little positive energy had been transferred to it. The hotel was very unfriendly, with a massive reception area similar to the impersonal departure lounge at Moscow Airport. Hundreds of tourists from outlying areas of the Soviet Union jostled with sightseers from Bulgaria and other eastern bloc nations. The reception desk was totally unhelpful, especially when trying to get a direct line to London or sorting out some currency problem. The breakfast room was like the interior of a dingy cathedral, with threadbare furniture. The same depressing menu was in evidence every day – boiled eggs, coleslaw and dry brown bread.

Upstairs, on each floor of the hotel, little old ladies sitting at desks were in charge of the room keys. Their stare was intense and they seemed to suspect every foreigner of trying to sneak a woman into their room. Women of ill repute were occasionally allowed to roam the curving corridors of the hotel, having bribed the relevant officials, but at the time of our visit, the hotel was on full alert. A prostitute had recently been found murdered and the authorities were on their mettle. In the basement of the hotel there was a prison cell to house any miscreants. It also provided a cooling-off place for those who had over-indulged in vodka.

Given this climate, the hookers had to make do with making their pitch at the back entrance to the hotel. They were a sorry crew – all dolled up in imitation furs, reeking of cheap perfume and strong cigarettes, which had stained their teeth. The best-looking of the bunch, however, were not so easily deterred. They managed to gain entrance to the night club or the basement floor. It was yet another contradiction; one of Soviet Communism's alleged show-case hotels blasting out the music of those denizens of Western society, Abba, with one of the oldest forms of capitalism in full swing.

Some of our intrepid *Newsnight* group made a couple of expeditions to the disco. The clientele was a motley collection of the aforementioned ladies of the night, pimps, drunken Russian businessmen, bodyguards, police informers and a number of gawping foreigners. It was like dancing in one of the most dangerous bars in the old Wild West of the United States – so it was a lot of fun for a while, though we did not linger long.

There were some advantages staying in the hotel, if you had the stamina to wander along a maze of corridors on the ground floor, past the bars intent on fleecing tourists out of their foreign currency. In a little cubby-hole tucked away from public view, I found a snack bar where you could buy blini and caviar in roubles, so we were able to have a feast for lunch for the equivalent of fifty pence. We certainly needed such treats, as our first film project involved editing round the clock for two days.

Away from the Cosmos, we could see that the standard of hotels was beginning to change, along with most other things in Moscow. We managed to have an evening meal at the aptly named Savoy Hotel, which had just opened in the centre of town. You had to pay in foreign currency at the hotel, which catered for wealthy businessmen. The Savoy's rooms cost a fortune and so were out of range of BBC expenses. However, the phones worked and there was comfort galore. In the dining room there was a grand piano and an extensive range of fine wines and cuts of meat – all a great contrast to the Cosmos. Other hotels were springing up, riding on the wave of joint ventures and capitalist enthusiasm.

While driving round Moscow, we often passed Dzerzhinsky Square, where the KGB had its headquarters. It was a weird feeling driving past this forbidding building which had witnessed so much brutality. During this trip we discovered that the reach of the secret police was evidently still very great. One of my initial ideas had been to interview a group of radical-leaning workers in the town of Zelecnograd on the outskirts of Moscow. It had been a closed area to foreigners because of the vast number of armament factories there.

We had met a group of the workers at an earlier protest rally in the centre of the city against Gorbachev's government. I had been drawn into the heart of their protest march and again had had to pinch myself. Could I really be among those taking part in such an open defiance of the communist system? Would we be fired on at any moment? But all had passed off peacefully and the

Zeleonograd contingent had given me their addresses. Peter Snow and I dutifully turned up a day or so later and were welcomed like long-lost relatives. Zeleonograd was a depressing, windswept place, especially at nightfall, and yet we took part in animated discussions in a small ground-floor flat where a group had gathered to discuss tactics. We arranged to come back the next day to do some filming. We thought the area was no longer closed and believed the protestors who told us we would have no problems.

However, early next morning I received a panic call from the organiser. The filming would have to be cancelled; she had been told by the authorities that we would not be welcome. Immediately, the spectre of the secret police had reared its head. I asked myself how they knew that we had intended to film there – was there an informer in the seemingly united group of campaigners? Was there a bug in our office? Had we been followed? Paranoia certainly breeds paranoia. I was obviously disappointed and alarmed by this news, but worse was to follow when I realised that we had arranged to meet the camera crew in Zeleonograd. They were in a different hotel at the time because the Cosmos was full.

I managed to get hold of Charles Wheeler, who told me that the crew had just left by car and it was not possible to contact them. I imagined the worst. What would happen? Would they be arrested? Deported? Imprisoned? I sweated for a couple of hours and then was mightily relieved when they arrived at the hotel. They had been stopped at a road block just out of Moscow and had been turned back. Again, I inwardly quaked at the power of the Soviet apparatus, though was glad nothing worse had happened. However, my credibility as the hot-shot leader of the group took a nose dive and it took a while before this particular crew were prepared again to go over the top for me.

Apart from this brush with the old-style control system, we managed to have relatively little to do with the Soviet authorities. However, we did get mixed up in a private enterprise which could have landed us in more trouble if it had gone wrong. One Sunday, we decided to take the afternoon off and go to Izmailovsky Park, where dozens of artists and street-sellers gathered. The range of goods on display was impressive, especially the religious icons and expertly decorated matrushka dolls – nattily painted wooden dolls of decreasing size which neatly fit inside one another.

It was a cold but sunny afternoon and consequently there were hundreds of buyers jostling for the best bargains. We had been given the nod that most traders were prepared – indeed, were keen – to accept dollars at reasonable rates. The only problem was that such black market activity was illegal and there were several Soviet soldiers on hand to try to stop such trading. There were also apparently a number of plainclothes policemen mingling with the crowd, ready to pounce on any foreigner who transgressed.

I am afraid the temptation was just too much for me, despite the risks. I had hardly any roubles on me. They were virtually worthless anyway and there was so much to buy. I especially liked one matrushka doll which had the figure of Gorbachev on the outside, minus the unflattering birthmark on his head. Inside was Raisa, the next powerhouse in the land, then in third place Yeltsin, the rising star. The hard-line communist Ligachev was next – but his doll was puny by this stage – and inside him was a tiny citizen, suggesting the powerlessness of the ordinary individual.

I was also intoxicated by the general atmosphere of risk, and increasing rebelliousness and daring. When I offered to pay in dollars, the elderly woman on the stall glanced around uneasily, then proffered her hand, which was clutching a disintegrating black mitten. What a strange custom, I thought; then I realised I had to put my dollars in the mitten and give it back to her. The transaction done, I walked off proudly with my prize. If anyone had been watching closely, it would have been so obvious what had been going on.

At another stall, a middle-aged man in a leather jacket nodded at me to follow him into a nearby copse of trees. By this time, I was feeling increasingly reckless and caught up in the thrill of the game; I duly followed him and we hid behind a tree, exchanging dollars for roubles. Moscow in 1990 was a lawless place where normal rules of civilised behaviour were breaking down and it was strangely liberating for us to cast off the norms of Western society for a while. However, it did seem incongruous that I behaved in such an ultra-capitalist fashion in the very cradle of communism.

There were yet more contradictions in store when I visited the parliament, the Supreme Soviet, which was beginning to flex its muscles as an independent power source. For one thing, despite being a foreigner and journalist to boot, it was relatively easy to get in. I managed to get a grandstand seat in the balcony to watch a special debate. I could not imagine a Soviet television crew having such an easy time trying to get into the chamber of the House of Commons. It was also an eye-opener to see the parliament using electronic voting techniques and displaying the results on a modern screen. There was nothing of our archaic parliamentary system of ayes and noes with tellers and lobbies. The Supreme Soviet looked much more like a modern democracy at work.

Even more surprises were to follow; we were allowed to do some vox pops in a corridor just outside the main debating chamber. Try doing that in Westminster and the Sergeant at Arms would eat you for afternoon tea! We found that the Soviet delegates were remarkably open and keen to talk. We did a quick interview with General Akhromeyev, the lean, balding former Chief of Staff of the Soviet Armed Forces. Little did we know that he would commit suicide within a couple of years, dismayed that the institutions he had devoted his life to had collapsed.

We did find one delegate somewhat reluctant to talk – Leonid Albalkin, Gorbachev's economic adviser. We didn't have a proper interpreter but Charles Colville, a London-based producer who was making great strides at learning Russian, accosted Albalkin and was determined to ensnare him. It was all to no avail; Albalkin slipped away quickly. It was only when he returned in a much friendlier mood a couple of minutes later that we realised that Charles' keenness had been preventing him from going to the toilet.

We were surprised to get so close to some of these

influential figures at such a crucial stage in Soviet history, none more so than the rising political star, Boris Yeltsin, who granted us an interview. Annoyingly, I could not go to the filming session because I was still editing our first film. It was a great regret, especially in the light of subsequent events, which saw him take over as the Russian President and make an indelible mark on the country's history.

Yeltsin had some forthright things to say in our interview when asked to assess the five years of Gorbachev's rule until that point. Yeltsin said the first two years had not been bad, but the rest had either been not very satisfactory or totally unsatisfactory. He said he was against Gorbachev's decision to push for seeking the powers of executive president and warned that he would have too much power, possibly becoming another Stalin.

"He loves power and he could use it without any limit," he growled. Yeltsin said he hoped that there would not be mass discontent and that the situation would be solved by parliament, but he warned that protestors could come out on the streets unless Gorbachev became more radical.

Despite all Yeltsin's hard-hitting verbal volleys, I had a tremendous battle to get the *Newsnight* editor, Tim Gardam, to agree to run the interview. The reason was one of those stupid turf battles that besets news and current affairs, and indeed the rest of the BBC; Yeltsin had been interviewed only rarely but had previously agreed to give an interview to Jonathan Dimbleby, who was making a special programme about Russia. Unfortunately, the special was to go out in a couple of days. The BBC powers-that-be felt *Newsnight* would be scooping the Dimbleby programme if our interview was broadcast earlier. For us, that seemed like madness; a news programme should reflect the news.

Both Peter and I rang London and complained bitterly. We were only saved by the fact that, unbeknownst to us, Yeltsin had already spoken to *Channel Four News* and they had now run their interview, so all silly talk of scoops and proprietorial disputes went out of the window. There was no option but to run our interview as soon as possible. We had wasted valuable time in arguing over this and Peter had got behind with his script for his in-vision links, which we were due to record in Red Square. We had hired a temporary hotel room near the Square but we had outstayed our welcome.

As Peter was finishing his intro, a determined hotel worker charged in and started chasing him down the stairs. Although Peter is very tall, this lady had the build of a wrestler and we had to meekly agree to pay an extra fee and clear off into the night. Outside was one of Vitaly's drivers, Valentine, who was not one of the brightest. We were in a hurry to drive to meet the crew at the far end of Red Square but it was like trying to warm up a corpse. While Valentine was fiddling with his keys and steering wheel, there was an almighty crash. The front seat – in which Peter was sitting rehearsing his lines – had collapsed, tipping him back until his neck rested on the back seat just alongside me. In a stunning display of unflappability and eccentricity, he carried on as if nothing had happened. As we lurched along in Valentine's hearse, Peter kept coolly talking to me about what he planned to say in the headline sequence. Peter would certainly have passed the apocryphal audition test talked about at the BBC, during which would-be news readers have the bottom of their trousers set alight to see if they can keep calm and continue to deliver their lines.

Throughout the trip, Snow's enthusiasm and eccentricities were a tremendous boon, especially while working in a difficult place such as Moscow, at a time of upheaval and uncertainty. His tendency to whirl his arms around and indulge in warm-up chat without embarrassment often made the difference between a tame interview and an animated one.

During our broadcasts from the Soviet Union, we hit on the idea of talking to four young people about their views of Gorbachev and the future. We recorded the discussion in the Rossiya Hotel, in a restaurant perched high above St Basil's Cathedral in Red Square, which was spectacularly lit at night. We encountered some problems as the interviews overran and we still had not finished when the restaurant opened. Many of the diners were open-mouthed at the spectacle. Unlike Western Europeans, they were still not yet used to the crazy demands that filming makes on the lives of normal individuals.

If they had understood English, the diners would have been quite surprised by some of the comments of the four youngsters – I certainly was. Three of them bemoaned the failure of the communist youth organisation, Komsomol, to address any of the problems or needs of young people. They were openly critical of the Soviet leadership for failing to provide any spiritual or moral direction. However, the establishment did have one champion in the fourth member of the panel, Igor Malyarov, a teacher dressed like an old fogey. He was loyal to the party line, which had kept the communist revolution going for the last seventy years.

Francine Stock also filed a fascinating film report about the changing face of Soviet youth. She tracked down one hotbed of dissatisfaction with the communist system – the 120 bodybuilding establishments in the Lyubertsy area of Moscow. In this suburb, sleek young men with finely-toned muscles were preoccupied more with an aggressive punk music lifestyle than they were with the pronouncements of Lenin. Their world view was personified by the hard, driving music of the Lyube band, who dressed up in military uniform to mock the authorities.

Attitudes were not just changing among the young. We decided to commission an opinion poll with *The Guardian* to sample the views of a cross-section of the population. It was one of the first opinion polls conducted in the Soviet Union. The science of psephology may have been in its infancy, but the Institute for Sociological Research was starting to gather an international reputation as a reliable and accurate pollster.

The Institute was situated on the outskirts of Moscow in a very drab area with monotonous blocks of flats everywhere. Rubbish was omnipresent, too; indeed, there were so many disgusting garbage tips on the streets and in apartment doorways that we considered making a short film called "The Dumps of Moscow." Another widespread feature of Moscow life at this time was the rickety lifts which haunted every apartment block. If the rubbish in the lobby didn't put you off visiting someone on the tenth floor, then the subsequent precarious journey in the escalator certainly did.

Fortunately, our discussions at the Institute were carried out on the ground floor at the office of Elena Bashkirova. She was an impressive lady of uncertain age with an impish sense of humour. Although she undoubtedly had notable scientific and commercial credentials, she would every now and then tip me a mischievous wink, especially when discussing sensitive questions about ideology.

The poll was conducted in six cities across the Soviet empire and provided an intriguing snapshot of the turbulence in the country's psyche. Gorbachev was still the most popular leader, maybe surprisingly so in the face of what we had found in Moscow. However, Yeltsin was closing the gap fast and Yegor Ligachev, the hardliner, came a poor third. The residents showed a considerable degree of liberal, independent thought on each question about Eastern Europe, disarmament policy and economic reform. Nearly 80 per cent approved the idea of private industry and nearly half said the Communist Party's leading role would disappear within five years. How right they were!

What was staggering about Moscow at the end of March 1990 was that nothing seemed to be beyond questioning. At the end of our trip, we witnessed a profound snapshot of the changing political landscape in the Soviet Union. It came in the form of an impassioned speech by a radical historian, Yuri Afanasiev. His comments occurred at the Congress of People's Deputies, which was debating Gorbachev's move to give himself those sweeping executive powers opposed by Yeltsin. In an unthinkable display of defiance, Afanasiev openly criticised Lenin. To gasps and howls of horror from astonished hard-line communists in the auditorium, he denounced Lenin as having instigated 70 years of state-sponsored mass violence and terror.

Afanasiev certainly livened up proceedings; he was eventually booed off the stage, though nothing worse appeared to happen to him. Was nothing sacred anymore? Although Gorbachev succeeded in getting his new executive powers at the end of the debate, it was clear that Afanasiev's bold display of glasnost had shown up the contradictions and tensions in the modern Soviet Union.

All in all, the trip had challenged perceptions about Soviet power and had thrown up some teasing questions. Could you imagine Stalin commissioning an opinion poll to see what the population felt about collectives? Why had Afanasiev not been immediately hunted down by a KGB death squad? Would Lenin have tolerated Yeltsin preaching such disobedience in the wings? In this fevered political climate, it was no wonder that even the weather seemed confused. The backdrop of thawing and thin ice seemed very appropriate for a communist edifice that was beginning to totter alarmingly.

CHAPTER THREE

South Africa –
Investigating The Third Force

The rise and fall of apartheid in South Africa has been one of the biggest international stories in my lifetime. As a *Newsnight* producer in the mid-eighties, my appetite had been whetted when I met the cerebral figure of Professor Dennis Brutus. He had been in prison at one stage with the legendary African National Congress figure Nelson Mandela on Robben Island, off Cape Town. Brutus was a man of dignified bearing, with a greying beard and vibrant, concerned eyes. He spoke with great passion yet tremendous authority.

Archbishop Trevor Huddleston, a prominent opponent of the apartheid system, was also a regular *Newsnight* interviewee during the mid-eighties, when the white South African government clamped down with such ferocity on black nationalists. He too was possessed of a strong moral force, which made his arguments compelling.

I was intrigued by this inner strength of the opponents of apartheid and was very keen to judge the moods and emotions of South Africa at first hand. The chance came in May 1991, when Tim Gardam wanted a producer to make three films with Julian O'Halloran, a veteran South Africa watcher. Naturally, I immediately threw my hat into the ring, ever keen to escape my managerial chores as deputy editor, such as having to draw up Jeremy Paxman's rota.

Flying to South Africa involved a long 11-hour overnight flight, but thankfully there was only a one hour time difference. Jet-lag was not that much of a problem but I was exhausted by not getting a decent night's sleep. That meant that my first view of Johannesburg was through bleary and blood-shot eyes. Much of the drive to the hotel in the Rosebank area was through prosperous streets with pleasant golf courses and garden walls covered with bougainvillea. What was striking though was the amount of security around some of the houses in the whites-only areas, with high walls, barbed wire, and many guards on patrol.

It all created a very uneasy feeling. Rosebank Hotel was very comfortable, though I did not have much chance to sample its delights. Within a couple of hours of landing I had met up with Julian and our South African fixer, Brenda Goldblatt, who were in animated conversation with a white activist from the ANC.

The iron law of successful filming abroad is to get a good fixer who knows the local political scene intimately and can take acceptable short-cuts. Brenda fitted the bill perfectly; she was a whirlwind of energy and knew many of the key characters on the South African stage. Already she was on the track of a story which was on the point of breaking in a big way. It was about the so-called Third Force, a shadowy body accused of fomenting violence in the black community. The debate about the activities of such a group had increased given the terrifying increase in politically-motivated killings in the townships. Many of the deaths had been caused by the escalating rivalry between the ANC and the mainly Zulu Inkatha movement, headed by Chief Buthelezi.

There was mounting evidence that this tension had been exacerbated by a group comprising hard-line white elements in the South African security forces. They had acted as agents provocateurs, and had been supplying arms and military know-how to Inkatha, which was considered more ideologically compatible because of its adoption of free market economic policies. While desperately trying to keep awake at this initial meeting, I agreed that the Third Force issue would be an excellent topic for our final film. We all knew it would not be easy and would take time, luck and investigative skill.

We had already decided that our first film would deal with the internal operations of the ANC, which were widely regarded to be chaotic and ineffective. This piece had to be done much more quickly, as time was limited. We felt that it would have to be a more theoretical, interview-based film, which meant that it could be finished in a few days. Given my previous exposure to impressive figures such as Dennis Brutus and Trevor Huddleston, I felt a little apprehensive about doing a potentially knocking film about the ANC. There was, though, no doubt that the ANC at that time was struggling to organise its activities properly. In addition, my BBC conditioning to be impartial also kicked in, so I happily threw myself into the project.

Julian had already fixed up an interview in Cape Town the next day with the apartheid government's Information Minister, Stoffel Van der Merwe. I had to shake off any fatigue from the London flight and soon afterwards we took the two-hour flight to the city of Table Mountain. We were met by Cliff Bestall, an imaginative cameraman and an impressive, cool operator. I did not see much of the city, as it was dark and stormy when we arrived. Our hotel was right by the beach but it felt more like the exposed east coast of England on a wet day in winter rather than the idyllic place conjured up by tourist guides to Cape Town. Ah well, I suppose it would have been different if we had arrived there in southern hemisphere summer rather than winter.

As it was, I only had fleeting glimpses of Table Mountain, as there was so much low cloud and rain. I could hardly grumble as I was not there on holiday and so counted everything as a bonus, including a quick drive out of the city to the Afrikaner University in the wine growing area of Stellenbosch. We went there to interview a leading political thinker in South Africa, Professor Sampie Terreblanche. He gave an animated analysis of the current state of the ANC's strategy and tactics. His basic conclusion was that the ANC had been successful as a protest movement but was now finding it difficult to institute suitable procedures to allow it to function effectively as a mainstream political party. His views were supported in an interview we did later with the Reverend Allan Boesak; he bemoaned the fact that the returning ANC exiles were refusing to co-operate with anti-apartheid campaigners like him, who had kept the flame alive during the years of Afrikaner repression.

After filming in the Cape Town area, I had to dash back to Johannesburg on discovering that Nelson Mandela, who had been released from prison less than 18 months previously, was going to give a press conference there the next day. We had also heard that an interview with the ANC's foreign affairs spokesman Thabo Mbeki was a strong possibility. Julian had to stay behind in Cape Town as the interview with the Information Minister had been delayed.

An opportunity to see such a massive political figure as Mandela in the flesh only comes rarely and I could not help but be excited by the prospect. However, the press conference nearly turned out to be a big disappointment. The great man had been detained while on a visit to an isolated village in the bush. The assembled crowds of hacks were growing restless, despite being provided with drinks to help assuage their impatience.

Even these grizzled, battle-hardened reporters were keen to see such a legendary figure as Mandela. Eventually, the chuntering press corps received its reward, when Mandela appeared two hours later. He was undoubtedly impressive, with an erect statesman-like bearing, dressed immaculately in a dark suit. He walked stiffly but in a dignified way to the microphone and talked cogently, though not in a particularly inspiring manner. He was asked several questions about the township violence and was very tough in his attitude to the South African leader, President de Klerk. Mandela was also greatly perturbed by the Third Force allegations, and condemned the agitators behind the scenes.

I tried hard to secure an interview with him but the ANC would not make him available. I was also pushed for time as I had to rush off for the interview with Thabo Mbeki, which had now come through. Normally, a reporter would have done the interview but in Julian's absence I had to take on the task. I usually enjoyed posing questions on the odd occasion when I had the chance, though was a little nervous about this encounter. Perhaps I had a sixth sense, as the Mbeki interview project nearly ended in disaster before it had even begun. I did not realise that there were two ANC offices in Johannesburg, and so went first of all to the wrong one. I then got lost on the streets of the city and ended up having to run about a mile to turn up at the right place, where Mbeki was waiting to do the interview. By the time I arrived, a little late, I was dripping in sweat, breathless and mightily embarrassed. Fortunately, the camera crew had arrived on time and had managed to hold the fort. The cameraman was Richard Atkinson, who lived in Johannesburg and did a lot of BBC work, so he had not been confused about the location. What he made of my panting appearance, goodness only knows.

Happily, Thabo Mbeki seemed entirely unfazed by the whole episode and the interview went off quite well. He dealt fluently with my questions about the ANC's poor organisation and I was impressed by his demeanour. At this time, he was being touted as a possible successor to Nelson Mandela and it was easy to see why. He was, of course, later to assume the South African presidency in 1999.

This first film about the record of the ANC also provided an opportunity to visit the large township of Soweto, with its reputation for violence, squalor and dissent. I was expecting to see mile after mile of shanty town but, in the event, I was surprised to see what appeared to be some reasonable suburbs with modern petrol stations and neat brick houses. On the face of it, many properties did not appear to be the hovels I had prepared myself to see. Having said that, even the better areas of Soweto were still far below the sumptuous standards of the white strongholds in Johannesburg, and the black population who lived in the township were denied economic opportunities and other basic freedoms.

During our visit we also saw some of the more squalid parts of the Soweto township. One section, Chicken Farm squatters' camp, was particularly depressing. It consisted of several dozen shacks made of corrugated iron, set among foul-smelling dirt streets. Some of the occupants had been the victims of a terror campaign by fire bombers. We interviewed one shack-dweller outside his house, which had been reduced to a tangled heap of blackened, smoking metal. These incidents were so common that the ANC told us that their local organisers in the Soweto area were suffering from stress and burn-out after only three months.

All this was very shocking, but I was also very alarmed by the general lawlessness throughout Johannesburg. The seemingly prosperous commercial centre of the city was deceptive, as there were numerous robberies and assaults, with visiting foreigners one of the main targets. During our three-week stay, I met two people who had been mugged at knifepoint.

There was also plenty of other anecdotal evidence around to suggest that these were far from isolated cases. On one Saturday evening, our fixer, Brenda, took me out for a night on the town. We poked our noses into a number of establishments from a disco to a nightclub to a jazz bar. One unforgettable pit-stop involved a visit to a hotel which had been at the centre of intrigue when four prominent white political figures had plotted some subversive and corrupt activities in what became known as the Muldergate Scandal. Now the hotel had a huge dance-floor with hundreds of heaving figures, virtually all of them black. There were many tall, sinewy women from other parts of Africa including Somalia, Kenya and Mozambique.

At the end of our memorable evening out and a couple of bars later, I was taken aback when Brenda airily announced: "This is the first time for ages I've been out in the city centre on a Saturday night without seeing a least one dead body in the gutter." For her, violent street crime was an inevitable and routine part of life – and she suggested heading for home before we witnessed the culture of violence too closely for ourselves.

I was not too pleased with the way the ANC film turned out; it had all been very rushed and the structure was rather awry. I was, though, extremely happy with the second film we did. It dealt with a small rural settlement called Magopa, which had been virtually dismantled after its lands were seized by the white minority government and its black occupants forcibly evicted. The villagers had obtained a land deed back in 1913 but this legal right was ignored by the government in the seventies, when houses were smashed down by bulldozers and the villagers beaten. Many were forced to settle dozens of miles away to the west in the so-called independent homeland of Bophuphatswana, known as Bop.

Some of the villagers had now started to drift back and challenge the apartheid authorities. Brenda and I travelled out there one Saturday afternoon for some initial research. Magopa is situated about a hundred miles west of Johannesburg on a plain near to the town of Ventersdorp, the stronghold of the extreme right-wing AWB organisation, led by Eugene Terreblanche. It was no surprise that in this hard line area the ownership of village lands aroused a lot of passion. Although it was surrounded by controversy, the area itself was one of the most tranquil places I have ever been to. Contented cattle roamed on the grasslands and a soft breeze whispered gently through the long grass. From Magopa you could see for miles across the savannah, with no obvious sign of civilisation.

The few families who had returned to Magopa were doing their best to restore their previous undisturbed pastoral existence. They had re-established the well and rebuilt some of the houses destroyed in the eviction. We met three of the village elders in a temporary corrugated iron shack and were treated with respect and friendship. They were not radical activists but determined people out to uphold their historical legal rights. They took us to the disused graveyard where their immediate ancestors were buried – a place of solitude and contemplation. We were also taken to the site of the former school which had been destroyed. The villagers were fighting their battles in the courts but at any moment expected a raiding party from the white farmsteads surrounding them.

Later, for the purposes of professional balance, we visited one of the nearby farms owned by Wilhelm van der Rot. Although we were treated with suspicion as foreign media, we were nevertheless made welcome as fellow whites. We were given a full tour, including visiting the school run for the black workers on the farm. The relationship seemed to be more like that of slaves and their masters, yet there was no obvious sign of any ill-treatment of the black workers. At lunch we were treated to an outdoor barbecue, complete with massive steaks and South African beer. The food was certainly plentiful and appetising – the conversation arguably less so. Wilhelm had invited several neighbouring families and we were regaled with tales of how terrible the country was becoming because of the increasing power of the black population. "South Africa will become just like the mess in Zimbabwe," they grumbled.

In the final section of the film we went to visit some former occupants of Magopa, who had been moved to Bop but had no intention of returning home. They had settled near the capital Mmabatho, close to the historic town of Mafeking. This appealed to our sense of imperial history and we avidly made a bee-line for the British fort, which had been under siege in the Boer War. We were to be disappointed; hardly any stones from the fort were still standing and the site was set on the smallest of hills. We did film in the nearby museum, which was run by an eccentric Brit who had made it his life's work to study Britain's colonial exploits in the region.

The new capital of Mmabatho was built largely on an economy of gambling and there was plenty of new construction work. However, much of the development was misguided and ruined by corruption, typical of all the so-called black independent homelands set up by the apartheid government of South Africa. We took a trip out of the capital, which proved to be even more instructive. On the road we criss-crossed in and out of South Africa proper; where there were healthy-looking fields, that was South African territory. At other points on the journey, the road cut through dusty plains with hardly any crops. That meant we had crossed back into Bop. Nowhere were the iniquities of apartheid better illustrated.

Being in this settlement was like being in an isolated third world environment. It was not a very welcoming place, as many of the black families we talked to were antagonistic, possibly to hide their guilt over accepting the financial inducements offered by the state to stay there. They showed little interest in returning to Magopa, preferring to lead a more quiet existence, albeit in less wholesome surroundings.

The third film on the trip – about the Third Force – was the hardest to make and contained the strongest material. It began with a sequence at a funeral of a factory worker gunned down in a massacre at a beer-hall in Sebokeng township, south of Johannesburg. For me, the pictures did not reflect the incredible emotion displayed at the funeral, which took place at the large sprawling municipal cemetery. At least thirty funerals were planned for that day, and graves for all the bodies had already been dug.

These were very close together and it meant that the terrain consisted of large mounds of dirt created by making the graves, interspersed with the deep holes for the coffins. Several funerals were taking place simultaneously, the coffins placed at regular intervals along the row of graves. Each funeral attracted a couple of hundred mourners, many of them uncontrollable in grief, swaying and singing subdued, penetrating tunes.

It was one of the most depressing occasions I have witnessed. All around, people were scrambling on the mounds of earth to get a view of a coffin being lowered or to throw a handful of soil onto it. I nearly fell into a neighbouring hole several times while watching the funeral we were filming. The singing for our victim was particularly haunting and I found it greatly moving. Most of the funerals scheduled for the day were for victims of political violence in the area. Sebokeng had been in the vanguard of ANC resistance against the apparatus of the apartheid state in the eighties. Now it was riven by a battle for turf between Inkatha and the ANC.

This rivalry had given rise to a series of random atrocities in the area, one being at the beer-hall, in which eight people were shot dead by two gunmen carrying AK-47s. We visited the beer hall, or shebeen, in local parlance, to film the scene of the massacre, and it turned out to be a demoralising experience. The building was like an unkempt barn, smelling of urine and alcohol. Inside the poorly-lit hall were bedraggled groups of wasters drinking locally-brewed beer out of buckets. It was hard to see why such flotsam and jetsam had been singled out for such a brutal assault. Presumably, the massacre had been designed as a terror tactic, and the blame was put on Inkatha as part of a campaign to destabilise the ANC organisation in the Sebokeng area.

The focus of the battle was at a large hostel in Sebokeng, which housed about five thousand black migrant workers. Supporters of Inkatha had allegedly launched a series of murderous raids in the previous few months and nearly two hundred hostel dwellers had been killed. There were claims and counter-claims about who was to blame for instigating firebomb attacks and shooting sprees.

We interviewed several ANC supporters there on a Saturday afternoon, at a time when people were lying around listlessly, far from their homes and families. They seemed unable to forge any meaningful activity from their scant leisure time. One or two women were sitting around the compound, girlfriends of some of the inmates who were trying to compensate for their missing families. The presence of these women was a source of fights and bitterness, and this added to the overall atmosphere of mistrust, suspicion and fear. The men's living quarters were tiny and dark, with few furnishings. The explosion of violence made an already miserable existence far worse. Some of the inhabitants were Zulus, who denied any allegiance to the political party of the Zulus, the Inkatha Freedom Party. We interviewed some of them, who claimed they were being victimised because they refused to join the IFP.

In response to this swirl of violence, the ANC in Sebokeng formed their own defence unit to patrol the grounds of the hostel. This was a very sensitive issue for the ANC; it could have led to claims that they were founding illegal private armies and complicated the argument over whether the ANC really was living up to its promise to give up the armed struggle. We had a stroke of luck and managed to get ourselves invited to a training session for this ANC defence unit. It took place under cover of darkness and was made even more eerie because all electric power had been turned off due to a widespread dispute over the lack of payment of bills. From a producer's point of view, it was a tremendous thrill to be welcomed into the inner sanctum. The display of physical fitness and military prowess was certainly intimidating, though it was not clear how effective it would be in actual battlefield conditions. For us, it was something of a coup to be able to record some of this clandestine session on video.

The blame for provoking the troubles in Sebokeng was placed on a nearby hostel in the grounds of a big industrial steel-making company. This hostel was inhabited by Zulus, who were mainly supporters of the IFP. We decided to take a look for ourselves and arranged to interview the party's local rep at the hostel. She was a feisty character, who had been hurling out a stream of accusations about the ANC. However, when we approached the gates of the hostel to film the interview, we were stopped by a couple of surly Zulus and told to wait. The situation was rapidly becoming very tense, so I tried some "football diplomacy" by joining in a game of heading with a few youths playing just inside the compound. Eventually, a compromise was reached whereby we could interview the IFP leader in front of the hostel gates. She certainly performed well for the cameras, if somewhat eccentrically. She claimed the deaths at the other hostel had been caused by ANC supporters hearing a noise in the night. They believed they were under attack and so had trained their guns on each other and in the confusion had shot themselves.

Just as the interview was coming to an end, we were interrupted by the arrival of a big truck containing a couple of white security guards from the company. They immediately came over to us and snarled that we were on private property and had better stop filming. They also demanded that we hand over our videotape to them so they could check whether any security rules had been breached. They promised that the tape would be returned to us if there was no problem. Of course, we knew and they knew that we would never see the tape again if we gave it to them, so it was a sticky moment. An argument raged for about twenty minutes, with Julian and I trying to muster as much righteous indignation as we could, saying that this was no way to treat BBC journalists.

The cameraman, Cliff Bestall, kept his cool throughout. You cannot be a cameraman in South Africa without knowing how to thwart over-eager security goons. In a sleight of hand which would have brought credit to a professional magician, he changed the tape we had recorded onto for a blank one, which he duly handed over. The tape with our material on it was safely secreted away under the back seat of our Kombi van. We swiftly made our retreat. We then took up station outside the perimeter fence and started to take a general shot of the factory complex, to show the location of the hostel. We were spotted by a different set of security men but on this occasion we saw them coming in time and had the chance to drive off.

Despite the lack of hospitality at this hostel, we nevertheless were back a few days later. This time we arranged to film with the police, who were escorting IFP members from the hostel to join a mass Inkatha rally at a football stadium in Soweto. The Zulus were in full cry and prepared for the gathering by whipping themselves into a ceremonial frenzy. The full assortment of cultural weapons was on display – assegais, pangas, shields, animal-skins and knobkerries, sticks fashioned out of tree branches with a fearsome round ball of wood at the end. We managed to sneak just inside the gates to film this and I had a lucky escape when following Cliff into a circle of kneeling Zulus. Suddenly, they leapt up with a loud bellow, thrusting their spears towards the sky, one of them narrowly missing my abdomen.

We then went on to film them being given a special cultural drink with a cannabis base. This was supposed to have mystical qualities to give Zulus a high before battles and to improve their performance as warriors. Such concoctions were apparently used in the nineteenth century when the Zulu hordes took on the British Army at Isandlwana and Rorke's Drift. The modern-day drinking ceremony was accompanied by chanting and singing, which produced such an overwhelming wall of sound that it must have rivalled the noise made by the followers of the great Zulu warrior king, Ceteshwayo.

These chaotic scenes were witnessed by members of government security forces safely huddled in their casspirs, forbidding armoured vehicles used for riot control. Their presence did little to dampen the ardour of the Zulus, adding to suspicions that these vehicles had escorted some of these same Zulus to some of their murderous raids on the ANC in Sebokeng in previous months. These allegations appeared to be confirmed by a former policeman, who told us on film in silhouette that he had personally witnessed police helping Inkatha supporters against the ANC. This was a powerful testimony and gave our film considerable credibility.

The rally itself passed off peacefully. It gave us the chance to see Chief Buthelezi and King Goodwill Zwelithini bedecked in full tribal gear, exhorting their cohorts to greater efforts. The crowd was further encouraged by a cheerleader who rolled around on the ground, doing somersaults and brandishing his spear and sword in menacing fashion. The cameraman, Cliff, was quite taken with this demonstration of fervour and physical prowess. He whispered to me that the Zulus were a thrilling people; it was hard to disagree, as it was very impressive to see such energy, which conveyed an aura of confidence and an indomitable sense of destiny.

At the time of making the film there was a huge fuss about whether the Zulus should be allowed to carry their cultural weapons. Nelson Mandela had been insisting that these weapons should be banned, otherwise negotiations over the country's future would be called off. For Buthelezi, this was not only a question of honour but also of cultural identity, which he claimed was under threat by the violence of the ANC. Eventually, President de Klerk managed to come up with a compromise which satisfied all parties. However, it was difficult not to conclude that the exuberant and outlandish showing off of these weapons must only have contributed to the tension between the two black groups, which had caused 1,500 deaths in the Transvaal region in just twelve months.

Not all Inkhata supporters were so threatening; we met a softly-spoken white lady, Suzanne Voss, who organised publicity for the IFP, and was on a recruiting drive to entice other whites to support Buthelezi. We went to her house in the rich white suburb of Sandton, in Johannesburg. This was a comfortable building with the ubiquitous high walls and security trimmings. Suzanne came up with an unforgettable line that white supporters of Inkatha in this area did not wave their cultural weapons – they just rattled their jewels.

We were keen to include some other sequences in the film and so decided to travel to Natal in the south east, where the violence between the ANC and Inkatha had originally erupted a number of years before. The violence was still continuing in several places and we chose to go to the Richmond area, close to the English-looking town of Pietermaritzburg. But the lawless situation was far from being like England, as the gun ruled in a number of surrounding villages. We were warned not to linger in these villages after nightfall and ensure that we were back over the river near Richmond before it was dark. Most of the scattered population of sixty thousand had fled and were in hiding, as bands of supporters of both the ANC and Inkatha regularly clashed in bitter, localised fire fights. It was very disconcerting moving quietly around the deserted dirt roads and stumbling across burnt-out schools and houses. On a narrow track leading up a hill, we encountered a church minister who was loading up his car with as many belongings as he could. He had stayed with his family as long as he had dared to try to help those devastated by the violence, but finally he had had enough.

As we interviewed him in his seemingly tranquil garden, an ominous cackle of gun-shots could be heard in the distance. As we penetrated further into the no-go zone, we came across a Christian mission situated on the crest of a hill, which gave a terrific view of the verdant valleys below. We met Reverend Roger Hudson, a white priest in his thirties who was full of courage, and was staying to protect the work of the mission – whatever the risks. He had witnessed fighting between rival gangs across the valley – much of it sparked off at a graveyard, when victims of previous encounters were being buried. Reverend Hudson was in despair. "Life has become a sequence of funerals," he said. "White youths go to the movies at weekends; black youths go to funerals."

The whole landscape looked beautiful as the sun shone over the rolling hills and fertile fields, but we were running out of patience with this desolate place. We pressed on just a little further to one settlement of ten thousand souls where nobody was visible at all. It was extremely unsettling. We filmed at a burnt-out house of an ANC representative who had been forced to flee after a firebomb attack.

All in all, it was a very depressing experience, with the unleashed forces of violence seemingly beyond anyone's control. We found evidence in this area that the violence had been fostered by white elements in the security forces. For us, the Third Force was a frightening reality. All of our allegations were later put to the Law and Order Minister Adriaan Vlok, who gave evasive and unsatisfactory answers. My main memory of his interview was not his words, but the department's slogan behind him: *We protect and serve.* It had a very hollow ring, and such hypocrisy made the deepest impression of all during my first exposure to the tangled web of South African power politics.

SOUTH AFRICA'S FIRST FREE ELECTION – 1994

Three years later, I was back in South Africa to organise a special debate just before the country's first post-apartheid elections in April 1994. The tension between Inkatha and the ANC I had witnessed on my first trip was still in evidence; Inkatha was threatening to boycott the election and it was feared that there could be widespread bloodshed after the poll. By this time, I had become the editor of the *Assignment* documentary programme and was asked by the then BBC2 channel controller, Michael Jackson, to produce a special discussion on the future of South Africa. The presenter of the debate was Michael Buerk, a former BBC correspondent in South Africa.

We decided to host the debate in the same courtroom in Pretoria where Nelson Mandela had been sentenced thirty years before. Among the panel members were the irrepressible anti-apartheid campaigner Archbishop Desmond Tutu and the white author and journalist Rian Malan. The mood was generally apprehensive about what might happen in the days after the election.

Our mission completed, we returned to London shortly before the election. By the time we got off the plane, an unexpected deal had been agreed between Inkatha and the ANC. The mood had switched to optimism, with Inkatha deciding to take part in the elections, and polling day itself was to be a triumph for peaceful democracy. Watching at home, I could hardly believe that this was the same country I had just visited, where pessimism had been so widespread. In my lifetime, this was certainly one of the swiftest and surprising moments of great change in global affairs. In my two trips to South Africa I had seen first-hand the misery caused by the apartheid system. Like everyone else, I realised there would still be a long road to travel before South Africa's many problems would be properly addressed, but there was no doubt that this had been a dramatic shift for the better.

It was to be another 11 years before I returned to South Africa, this time to watch the England cricket team play the Springboks. By 2005 there were signs of impressive economic progress – in the area between Pretoria and Johannesburg, a myriad of modern offices and hi-tech developments had now sprouted. However, a variety of social, political and economic inequalities remained; Johannesburg was as dangerous a city as ever for the visiting tourist, but I was glad to see that the days of apartheid were definitively over. It was very inspiring to listen in person to the new joint national anthem, which now blended the sweet tones of the Xhosa hymn *Nkosi Sikelel' iAfrika* with the dour, white nationalist anthem of Die Stem.

CHAPTER FOUR

In The Land of Milk and Honey

After more than ten years dealing with international news, I had become increasingly aware of a substantial gap in my experience of one of the world's biggest and longest running stories: the conflict in the Middle East. This is a region which has always fired the imagination, with tales over the centuries of intrigue, religious fervour and romantic deserts. Since the creation of Israel as a modern state in 1948, the stakes in the area had obviously become much higher. Throughout the eighties on *Newsnight*, we mounted endless in-depth panel discussions (known affectionately in the trade as "gropes") following the twists and turns of the peace process. One frequent Israeli visitor to the *Newsnight* studios during this period was Benjamin Netanyahu, who years later was to become prime minister of his country. It was always very frustrating producing these items, as so often the characters involved – including Netanyahu – would revert in a blinkered way to merely stating their public hard-line positions. I was well aware that this was a region where you had to dig much deeper and get beyond the over-used rhetoric to have any chance of understanding the issues involved.

By the summer of 1992 I had itchy feet again. I was desperate to escape the shackles of the office and my deputy editor managerial duties, so when I realised that an election in Israel was coming up in June, I lobbied hard to go. Tim Gardam was sceptical of devoting too many resources to covering the poll. As he quite rightly pointed out, most Israeli elections usually ended in a toothless PR-induced stalemate, involving a bewildering array of tiny religious and secular parties, as well as the better known Likud and Labour parties. This time, though, I latched on to predictions that the left-leaning Labour party, under the veteran war hero Yitzhak Rabin, could definitively wrest away power from Yitzhak Shamir's right-wing Likud party. Such a victory would mean a possible breakthrough in the peace process with the Palestinians. I managed to convince Tim that this was at least a strong possibility, so he sanctioned a full bells and whistles trip. We planned to have a live studio transmission on election night, presented by that master of the polls, Peter Snow.

It had been a while since I had been away with Peter and I relished the prospect of accompanying him to the Middle East, one of his specialist areas. Planning for the trip was the usual battle between wanting to be well-prepared while coping with the day-to-day demands of getting *Newsnight* on the air. We did manage to draw breath occasionally in Peter's office and pore excitedly over a number of large-scale maps of the area he had stashed away. The main focus was on the question of land for peace and the clear difference between the two main parties over future negotiations with the Palestinians. Rabin was prepared to make several territorial concessions; he also took a relatively hard-line about the creation of new Jewish settlements on the West Bank. He wanted to freeze all new development, a view shared by the American government, which was threatening to withhold billions of dollars in loans if Shamir continued his intensive settlement programmes in the occupied territories.

Many colleagues made me aware of the special problems of working in Israel among two polarised communities. It was therefore vital to find and work with two excellent fixers, one Jewish, and one Palestinian. The Jewish part of the equation was fulfilled by a rambunctious film producer called Israel Goldvitch, a keen practitioner of the Jewish orthodox faith. He had become legendary in BBC circles for his gift of the gab. He also had the reputation for delivering the goods, though some considered him to be too much of a handful. I spoke to him a couple of times on the phone from London and had no hesitation in hiring him.

With his ceaseless wheeling and dealing, and constant use of the mobile phone, Israel was to secure interviews for us with both Shamir and Rabin, as well as being an inexhaustible fund of vital local knowledge. We could not have managed without him.

The Palestinian fixer, Hakam Fahoum, was a complete contrast. He was tough yet laid back; political not spiritual. I could not penetrate his psyche at all, whereas Israel often wore his heart on his sleeve. Occasionally, we had to travel together with both these different characters, as we went to both Jewish and Palestinian areas on the same day. Fortunately, professional considerations overcame any political and ethnic tensions.

Travelling around the West Bank as a foreign film crew was particularly difficult. If you travelled in a vehicle with the yellow number plates of the state of Israel, there was a good chance it would be stoned by Palestinian activists. If you travelled in a vehicle with the red number plates of the local Palestinian administration in the West Bank, it would be regarded with great suspicion in the areas near to Jewish settlements. It could well be frequently stopped by Israeli army patrols. Our solution was to hire a minibus from Hakam with Israeli number plates but with Arabic lettering on the outside bodywork. Our hope was that it would be taken for a vehicle belonging to one of the many Arabs legally settled in Israel itself.

Despite this, there was always some risk while travelling round Palestinian areas of the West Bank, so whenever we approached one of these places, Hakam would fish under the dashboard and stick a big sign on the window in Arabic lettering, saying we were from a Palestinian film company. Israel, who usually wore the traditional skull-cap – a kippah – would hastily cover his head with a flat workman's cap and pretend to be a lighting man.

As soon as we entered a Jewish settlement on the West Bank, there would be another frenzy of activity. Down would come the Palestinian film company sign and off would come Israel's unfetching cap to reveal his kippah. Israel would then assume an air of confidence; by contrast, Hakam would sink into his seat and pretend to be an Arab lackey.

We flirted with disaster after setting off from our hotel in Jerusalem on an early morning trip to the West Bank.

Hakam's driver was very late in picking us up, so we dived instead into a couple of taxis with Israeli number plates. The drivers were very reluctant to take us to the West Bank but said that they were prepared to have a go if we trebled the fare. We had little option but to pay up. The journey provided us with a real sense of what it was like to travel in an enemy's territory. The drivers were cagey and under stress throughout. Despite the earlier financial inducements, they would not take us the whole way down a track off the main road. They insisted on dropping us off the moment they spied a group of Palestinians in the distance. It was difficult for us to remain even-handed. Whatever actions we took could be interpreted wrongly by one side or the other.

For instance, we had a lengthy debate about which hotel we should stay in. The classic western media watering hole was the elegant American Colony Hotel in the eastern part of Jerusalem, which was heavily populated by Arabs. Staying there could be frowned on by Israeli contacts, as it would be seen to be siding with the Arab cause. Despite this, I was keen to stay there as the hotel had a reputation for exquisite decor, succulent food and historical connections. However, I was persuaded to stay instead in the draughty, modern Hilton Hotel in western Jerusalem. This was more convenient for driving out to Tel Aviv, as well as keeping Israeli contacts onside. However, staying there later did create some suspicion among some of our Palestinian contacts, who thought we were supporting the Israeli cause.

We did manage to fit in a fleeting visit to the superb American Colony Hotel, with its sumptuous courtyards.

No wonder that, 15 years later, Tony Blair was keen to base his office there for several years while acting as the Middle East Representative for the Quartet – the United States, Russia, the UN and the EU.

Like other *Newsnight* foreign trips, this visit to Israel necessitated much running around as we tried to produce a combination of pre-packaged films and live studio discussion programmes. Peter and I worked for the first few days on a piece about the Jewish settlements in the middle of the West Bank. For this, we had to find the right settlement in the right area with the right number of fluent-English speakers. It was a considerable challenge. Our search began south east of Jerusalem in the settlement of Tekoa, where the Old Testament prophet Amos had lived and had talked of a land flowing with milk and honey. The recce there proved to be rather tame, though it did give us the chance to drive through Bethlehem on the way back. Sadly, there was no time to stop, and we hardly saw anything as we encountered a torrential downpour. We had a quick glance at the famous square, the supposed site of Christ's birthplace, but my main memory of this sight-seeing opportunity is of pock-marked roads with streams of rainwater running down them and the local population scurrying for shelter.

We changed our search to the north of Jerusalem, where we struck lucky in another area of deep biblical significance. We visited the settlement at Beit El – or Bethel, as it was known in the Old Testament – where Jacob had a dream in which God announced to him that the people of Israel would be given the Promised Land. Beit El was also very relevant to the election issue of rights to land in the West Bank. The modern day settlement had a number of lively characters who fitted the bill for an informative and entertaining film. As a bonus, we discovered that a Palestinian family lived in a house next to the perimeter fence of the settlement. Beit El was expanding rapidly and it was clear that soon this Palestinian house was going to be virtually surrounded by Jewish buildings. The symbolism was too good to miss and so, accompanied by Hakam, I knocked on the door of the house to ask for permission to film.

The owner was a 51-year-old man called Khaled Kawaldi, who had eleven children with another one on the way. The house was quite large but had hardly any furniture and was flanked by a scruffy dirt yard full of rusting scraps of metal and scrawny chickens.

Khaled could hardly contain his brooding anger about the expansion of the Beit El settlement from fifteen to five hundred families in the space of a few years. "It is creeping like a cancer," he raged. He claimed his house had been stoned by youngsters at the Jewish settlement to try to intimidate his family and make them leave. This he adamantly refused to do. Khaled was very hospitable to us and his gang of young children was very well-behaved as we filmed them eating a simple meal.

The Jewish settlers of Beit El were equally welcoming and just as determined. They denied threatening Khaled and were immovable in their defence of the settlement policy. We filmed the settlement's children singing lilting Jewish songs at school and went on a dawn patrol in a jeep around the perimeter wire. We were also introduced to a quiet 35-year-old rabbi whose face had been badly burned in a Palestinian car-bomb attack a few years earlier.

Our film began with the sequence of a coach carrying school-children to Beit El from another smaller Jewish settlement five miles away. In the middle of the road through the militant Palestinian village of Ramallah was a continuous yellow line. This was a guide to Israelis driving in the area and was a warning to settlers not to stray from the route. The coach had to go right through Ramallah, where a couple of years earlier an Israeli woman and a couple of children had been killed when their coach came under attack. All this trading of hatred and violence had taken place in beautiful rolling countryside with fertile valleys. It was yet another assignment for me when it was hard to comprehend the cruelty unleashed by both sides locked into deep-seated political disputes. Whatever the rights or wrongs of the Israeli settlement policy, it was still shocking to see children anywhere having to be provided with an armed military escort on their way to school.

The urbane, impressive Palestinian negotiator, Hanan Asrawi, lived in this area and we were able to secure an interview at her house. Hanan was a small yet authoritative figure, attended by a couple of dedicated staff. She wore a smart suit with a purple shirt and treated us with courtesy. Behind the polite smiles, there obviously lurked steel; when the interview began, she poured scorn on the land polices of Rabin, as well as Shamir.

Hanan posed as big a problem for the Israelis as any car-bombers, militant gunmen, and student activists. A woman of such persuasive lucidity and logic went down very well with the international community and her presentation skills significantly boosted the Palestinian cause. She was a considerable agent of change. In Arab culture, it is unusual for a woman to have gained such political influence and it was hard not to be impressed by her inner strength and dignity. It was also a memorable experience to interview this sophisticated woman on the balcony of her house, with the noises of everyday life wafting up from the valley below – barking dogs, arguing children and wood-chopping.

To give our film some clout, we needed a spokesman from Likud, and so chased Ariel Sharon, one of the leading figures in the party pressing for a hard-line expansion policy. We missed him on a couple of occasions but ensnared him later in an election walkabout. Sharon, who later in life was struck down by a stroke which left him in a permanent vegetative state, was then a great bull of a man. He had a loyal, excitable band of followers, given his status as one of Israel's war-heroes. As Peter Snow grabbed an interview with him on the hoof, it was perhaps easy to see how the fledging state of Israel had managed to gain a foothold in such a hostile area. "It is all a question of life and death," Sharon snarled at Snow's testing question about whether seizing land from Palestinians could be justified.

The short interview nearly turned out to be a disaster because the main microphone failed and Sharon was picked up only on the feeble camera microphone. We just about got away with it on air but again this was another frustrating example of how being present at an actual event was much more exciting than what was later transmitted on screen.

Our film was shown three days before the election and went down well. We did though run into some flak from the *Panorama* programme, because they had a big film about Israel going out two days after our film. Unknown to us, they had also done a couple of interviews in Beit El and had spoken to Hanan Asrawi as well, so they were very miffed, as they felt we had been deliberately trying to spike their guns. We had not of course, but again it was another example of the competitive BBC, where you needed to show more diplomatic skills to mollify another programme than to deal with touchy protagonists involved in an international conflict.

Over the weekend before the election, we were able to snatch a few hours of down time from our hectic work schedule and headed for the coast near Tel Aviv. It was

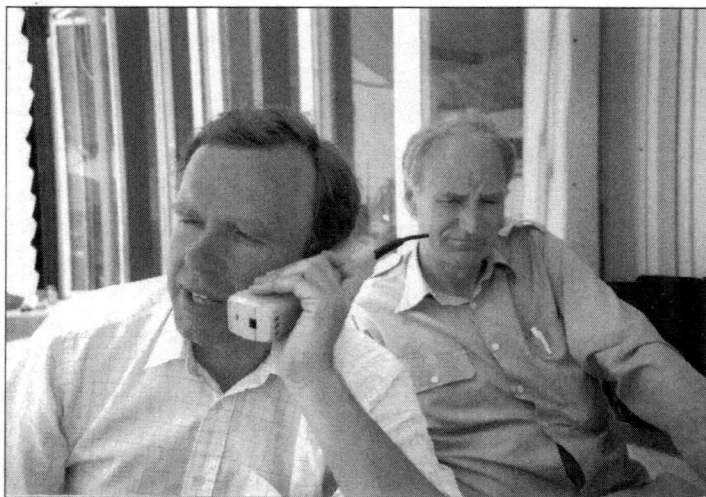

Wish you were here?
With Peter Snow during our Israel adventure.

delightfully warm and we basked in the sea and wolfed down a meal of local fish at the quaint and picturesque port of Jaffa. Peter had a mobile phone so we dialled up Tim Gardam at his home in Oxfordshire, ostensibly to discuss what our next contribution to *Newsnight* should be. However, I guess we just wanted to gloat at our good fortune at being in the sun. Being a television journalist has its frustrations, along with most professions; it can involve incredible stresses and pressures with long hours, but there are few occupations which can provide the chance to laze on a Mediterranean beach for free.

The break did not last long enough and soon we were on our way to a Saturday evening rally, where the main speaker was Yitzshak Shamir. Our fixer Israel had worked wonders as usual, and we had been promised a quick interview with Shamir afterwards. So, sated with sunshine and culinary delicacies, we set off in good heart. We arrived early so we could work out the best camera angles for shooting the speech. The rally was held in a square in a suburb of Tel Aviv. We negotiated with the owners of a local high-rise flat to let us film from their balcony and capture a dramatic wide shot of proceedings. Unfortunately, the rally turned out to be a drab, low-key affair and typified the ebbing fortunes of Likud. Shamir's speech appeared to be a catatonic ramble but he still had the capacity to rouse the faithful. At the end he was cheered heartily – albeit by a sparse crowd.

We moved in swiftly to grab a word with Shamir as he left the podium. I was especially pumped up for this encounter as I had to operate the battery light, one of the extra tasks for a producer now that specialist lighting assistants were being phased out. The light was needed to enable us to get a shot of Shamir walking along with his bodyguards in the gathering darkness. It was very difficult keeping his face lit properly, as his tiny frame was dwarfed by his much larger protectors.

Unfortunately, when we caught up with him he simply waved us away, saying he was too tired to give an interview. Although he was 77, we were dubious about his reason to remain silent. As a former leader of the Stern Gang, which opposed the British in the run-up to Israel's independence, Shamir apparently had never been fond of the BBC. He may also have recognised the towering figure of Peter Snow, with whom he had crossed swords in a bad-tempered interview a few years previously in the aftermath of the kidnapping of the Islamic cleric, Sheikh Obeid.

Israel came into his own in such adverse circumstances like these; he was on the phone immediately to demand another chance to interview Mr Shamir. His staff promised to give us another doorstep opportunity on the next day, though it would have to take place in the port of Haifa, way to the north. In the event, I stayed behind in Jerusalem while Peter and the crew chased Shamir around Haifa. Because this was an unexpected addition to the schedule, it meant the crew had worked a 22-hour day by the time they returned to Jerusalem in the early hours. This was the flip side to having briefly lazed on the beach the previous day. The doorstop with Shamir did not produce any riveting words of wisdom, but it lasted long enough to show his indomitable will and resolute refusal to consider any territorial compromises.

The brief interview took place after Shamir had laid a wreath in memory of members of the Stern Gang who had died fighting for their cause. While the Israeli anthem was playing, a fly landed on Shamir's nose. Rather than brush it away and destroy the dignified solemnity of the moment, he continued to stand motionless, apart from screwing up his nose to try to dislodge the troublesome insect. It made a telling metaphor for his steadfastness in times of adversity.

The other Yitzhak, Rabin, also gave us an interview. This again was a scrambled affair involving Israel chasing various top-level party apparatchiks. We eventually cornered our quarry at a hotel reception in Jerusalem, where the main feature of the event was watching a recorded television debate between Rabin and Shamir. Rabin sat chain-smoking throughout the screening and shifted nervously at intervals when it appeared Shamir had got the better of him. Whatever else, it made absorbing television, with good close-ups of Rabin's face – he spent most of the debate scrutinising his own performance and that of his opponent.

I again had to be in charge of the battery light for the interview, so it was hard to take in too much of the content. Instead, I was preoccupied with making sure ungainly shadows did not pass across Rabin's craggy features. When I watched back the exchange, I realised I hadn't missed much; he spoke in a dreary monotone and said little new, although he did make it abundantly clear that he was prepared to deal with the Palestinians. He said it was vital to have a change of atmosphere and take a risk in the search for peace. Because our latest film contained interviews with the two leaders, I should have been happy. Neither, though, delivered riveting television and once again I mused on the dilemma that television journalists face. There can be a macho tendency to always want to put the top people on camera but often more insight for the viewer can be provided by interviewing more articulate and lively people a little further down the pecking order, who usually have more freedom to tell it as it is.

The clash between these two veteran opponents became the spine of our second film, which went out on the eve of the election. We also tracked down some of the rival adverts made by the two camps and these contained strong personal attacks. Much was made of Rabin's alleged problems with alcohol and his uncertain mental health. Likud dredged up events from the 1967 war, when Rabin was Chief of Staff of the Israeli Defence Forces and disappeared from command for a couple of days, apparently suffering from a suspected nervous breakdown. One graphic advert had Rabin's face in a frying pan, slithering around like a yo-yo. "He is the non-stick leader," the commentary proclaimed. "He cannot be trusted, he is unstable."

In retaliation, Labour produced an advert with film of a monumental row between Shamir and Sharon at a Likud party meeting two years previously. The message was clear. Who would want to trust leaders who shouted insults at each other in public? The pictures were accompanied by Russian subtitles, in an attempt to woo the newly-arrived immigrants from the former Soviet Union.

Despite this lively television campaign, I feared the election would end in another parliamentary stalemate.

Had I sold a pup to my editor, saying that this election would be of historic importance? Would the election have any relevance to a British audience, if there was to be no real change in the Israeli approach to the peace process?

I need not have worried. On polling day we were planning for electoral gridlock; however, as the night progressed, we were given a tremendous shock when the exit polls indicated that Labour and its left-wing allies, the Meretz group, would win an outright majority. Suddenly we had a story. There were only two hours to transmission and we had to change tack quite considerably. I had already arranged an over-ambitious way of dealing with the election aftermath, believing I could introduce a lot of tricks I had learned while supervising the whole of the BBC's outside broadcast coverage for the British general election just a few weeks before.

I had organised two live outside broadcasts from both party headquarters and had a live studio in Tel Aviv, as well as Jerusalem. We had to rely on a local facilities house, which had a good technical reputation but had done little on this scale before. I only had the help of another producer, Amanda Farnsworth – who later became one of the masterminds behind the BBC's Olympic coverage in 2012 – and a studio director, Peter Day. The breaking story about a possible Labour win put extra pressure on these production limitations. I could tell we were in for a bumpy ride as we struggled to write and circulate all the scripts in time for the technical crew to prepare extensively.

In fact, the entire transmission was heading for a total disaster. We couldn't get the autocue working; the lines from Tel Aviv went down; we couldn't get sound from the winning Labour headquarters; and we couldn't establish a proper sound line from London. I therefore had to stand in the small, crowded, noisy gallery, talking to London by phone and passing on instructions directly into Peter's earpiece.

We also had a delicate political problem, as the Likud Health Minister, Ehud Olmert, had agreed to appear on the programme, provided he had nothing to do with a Palestinian spokesman whom we had booked earlier. Unfortunately, we could not bring Olmert into the programme at an early stage as he was in Tel Aviv, where the lines had failed. Although the Palestinian spokesman was already in the wide shot in the Jerusalem studio, we could not introduce and talk to him first – Olmert would have walked out if he had had to make his contribution after the Palestinian reaction had been given. I got caught up in a lot of these conundrums while working on *Newsnight*, especially when having to negotiate between interviewees from the British political firmament.

Because of my baptism of fire during the British election programme, I was just about able to keep my cool amid all this chaos and upheaval. However, I did nearly burst a blood vessel while having to yell at the local engineers to get their fingers out. Peter Snow held the show together magnificently and I was reasonably pleased with the transmission. As so often was the way, it felt a lot worse behind the scenes than it appeared to the viewer at home.

A lot of excitement about the historic result was generated by our reporter Michael Macmillan, who had broadcast with verve and panache from the Labour headquarters. It was only later that I discovered he could hear nothing in his ear-piece. He had had to be cued by a producer laying at his feet and tugging his trouser leg when it was time to begin. My main reaction afterwards was one of relief. It could have been yet another escapade which could have led to the sack and oblivion. In my hotel room afterwards, I wondered why I carried on with such a job which involved sailing so close to the wind so often. But then, I thought, isn't that the fun of it? Live broadcasting always involves a risk, even as the equipment grows ever more sophisticated. It remains the most enjoyable and thrilling aspect of television production.

We had not been due to broadcast the next day and so had been looking forward to a leisurely start; this was ruined by the unexpected ground-breaking result. At 9am

The two of us on a research trip to the West Bank

I got a phone call from Tim demanding a long piece for that night's show. He had got his revenge for our gloating call from Tel Aviv beach which had disturbed his weekend. Instantly I shot off to break the news to Peter whose hotel room was a complete shambles. There were papers scattered all over his bed and the remnants of two food trolleys were stacked in the corner of the room, with Snow himself wandering around wearing just his underpants. From this chaotic base camp, he immediately called up the aides of Shimon Peres. He had an animated conversation about the result and put in a request for an interview.

Overall I was very pleased with the trip. Even the unexpected piece we had to do on the day after the election went reasonably well. I sent Amanda and Peter to another militant Jewish settlement, Ofra. Again they discovered feisty, determined characters, who were immovable in their wish to expand the settlements. Many of the more articulate and outspoken advocates of expansionism were middle-aged women who had at least eight children each. Such characters exerted mighty influence in the tortuous negotiations in the peace process. Snow had some fun with Shimon Peres by probing him on his obvious antipathy towards his party colleague, Rabin. Peres was unabashed – "Do you know any government where members of the cabinet form a love story?" he asked. Fair comment.

There are few joyous experiences like unwinding after a successful foreign trip. On the next day, we had a free afternoon and this time seized the opportunity to wander round Jerusalem. In this confusing and fascinating city, we could once again witness the determination and inflexibility that lies behind all religious disputes. We climbed the steps to the top of the church of the Holy Sepulchre, where a small community of Ethiopian Coptics was living in virtual squalor on the roof. Their descendants had been pushed out of the main church in an intra-denominational dispute over rights to land where Christ is said to have been buried. This squabbling between Christians was yet another indication of how difficult it would be to get any sort of peace in the highly charged religious atmosphere in the Middle East.

I also found it ironic, in the light of the high-profile disputes in the region between Jew and Arab, that the various Christian denominations at the Church of the Holy Sepulchre had entrusted the keys of the place to an Arab family to ensure fair play. I pondered this incredible fact as we flew home from what had been an engrossing and intriguing first-hand view of a land brimming with historical transformation. But, as subsequent years have shown, achieving substantive and lasting change in the Middle East is quite another story.

CHAPTER FIVE

Rescue Mission in Yemen: Pawns in a Power Game

For more than a decade the tiny country of Yemen has been known as something of a breeding ground of terrorism in the Al-Qaeda mould. My only visit to the country came in 1998, just as Yemen was emerging on to the international stage. At this time the country was in the news because some tribal groups outside the capital, Sana'a, were beginning to kidnap foreigners to use them as a bargaining chip to try to improve their living conditions.

A team from the *Correspondent* current affairs show was sent to Yemen to report on this phenomenon. I had been the founding editor of *Correspondent* between 1994 and 1997, and still had some overall managerial responsibility for the programme at this stage.

The *Correspondent* team despatched to Yemen was made up of a cameraman, Frank Smith, a producer, Robin Barnwell and a reporter, Rageh Omaar, who was to become famous for his reporting of the toppling of Saddam Hussein in 2003. The team wanted to travel outside Sana'a to film some of these rebel tribes and were given permission to do so by the Prime Minister, Dr Abdul Karim al-Iriyani. At the last minute, the interior ministry intervened and warned that the safety of the team could not be guaranteed. But the team members set off nonetheless, knowing they had the support of the prime minister and believed that it was down to them to assess and take the risk.

In the event, the team's trip to the area controlled by the Bani Dhabyan tribe was a success and totally safe. However, on their way back into Sana'a, the three BBC men were arrested by government troops for allegedly breaking the law. It seemed that factions loyal to the President, Ali Abdullah Saleh, had a different perspective to the prime minister and were determined to make a point. The journalists were stopped at a checkpoint by up to 60 soldiers, armed with automatic weapons. Two heavy cars with mounted machine guns accompanied the troops. The journalists were treated roughly and faced tough questions.

Any arrest of BBC journalists overseas was always a matter for great concern and grabbed the attention of the bosses. This time there was an extra complication, as a team from the BBC *World Service* was also on the ground in Yemen, carrying out some test transmissions as a prelude to establishing an FM station. It seemed that their safety and mission might now be compromised.

With my management hat on, I was soon drawn into this unfolding crisis. It rapidly became clear that BBC current affairs needed someone on the ground who knew the three journalists and could help facilitate their release. I was lined up for the task and was anxious to get out there as soon as I could. I knew it would not be easy. Even at this stage, Yemen was regarded as one of the most heavily armed countries on earth, with an estimated three Kalashnikovs per head of population. I also knew it would be tricky to keep good relations with my colleagues from Bush House, who had been alarmed that their ambitious plans in Yemen had been put in jeopardy by our team's sense of journalistic adventure. My contacts in Yemen would be the head of the Arabic service, Gamon McLellan, and a senior member of the department, Hassan AbuAllah. I also worked very closely with my successor as the editor of *Correspondent*, Fiona Stourton, who had commissioned the Yemen report.

It took a while to convince the Yemeni authorities in London to give me a visa, but after a couple of days they agreed, provided I went as a manager and did not attempt to undertake any journalistic activity. I took advantage of the delay to contact a psychologist who had experience of debriefing western hostages after their release from places such as Lebanon. He warned me to be aware that the team might be nervous about a senior manager coming into such a situation and advised me to work hard at making them feel relaxed and supported.

By the time I was ready to leave London, we heard that the team had been transferred to an upmarket international hotel in Sana'a and was effectively being held there under house arrest.

I kept a diary of the ensuring trip to Yemen, which proved to be one of the most bizarre experiences of my professional life. The extracts which follow run over the next two chapters.

WEDNESDAY 3 JUNE 1998

When the Yemenia flight arrives in Sana'a at 4.45am, I look out for any security men who might be watching me. I fear that I might be held up by a passport official but he is very efficient and polite. I see a Ministry of Information sign and a minder leads me to a four-wheel station wagon. The trip into town is low key. Some of the suburbs look rundown, with many people milling around on the pavements.

The Taj Sheba Hotel receptionist is also courteous and she hands me a note from Robin saying he will see me later in the morning. It is signed Misses Smith, Barnwell and Omaar, a jokey reference to the initial incorrect reports that the team had been dressed up as women when they were arrested. I am glad to see they are keeping a sense of humour, but feel the note could be incriminating if it is read by the authorities, so I tear it up immediately in my room and flush it down the loo.

The room is very comfortable and I munch nervously on a banana from a bountiful bowl of fruit on the table. I write a note for Robin and co. to meet me at 8.15am. I ring the Sheraton Hotel and leave a message for Gamon to ring me at 8am. I am keen to get going as soon as I can, as not much happens after noon in Yemen. By then, it is becoming too hot and the qat chew is starting. Qat is a bitter-tasting, green-leaf narcotic which is widely consumed in Yemen, causing mood swings from euphoria to depression.

I have forgotten my toothbrush so clean my teeth with my finger. My room is number 605, one floor directly above the guys. Obviously we are in the "monitored" section of the hotel. I put the chain on the door and feel a little safer.

I eventually get to bed at 6.30am, knowing I will only get 90 minutes sleep.

The alarm goes off at 8am. I am very tired as Gamon rings immediately, right on cue. I arrange to meet him and Hassan. The three guys under arrest arrive at 8.30am and are delighted to see me. I follow the advice I was given in London by a psychologist and make it clear that everything that happens will be off the record. I tell them I am determined to get them out and but I will smooth over things with Gamon and the World Service. The three of them are delighted with the books I bought for them in London. They include *The History of Poland* by Timothy Garton Ash, *Fermat's Last Theorem*, *Captain Corelli's Mandolin*, *Birdsong*, *The Lonely Planet Guide to Yemen*, and *Mukiwa* by Peter Godwin, a former reporter on the BBC *Assignment* programme, the forerunner of *Correspondent*.

I tell them I am one hundred per cent working for their release; I have no other motives or obligations. I try to calm any resentment the guys may have against the Bush team. I explain the Bush staff are operating under different pressures but they are doing all they can, despite these constraints.

I say we have to assume we are being monitored and listened to everywhere we go in the hotel. The guys express some anxiety about the impact of their arrests on their jobs/contracts and the programme budget. I say not to worry at all and stress how important it is to keep totally together as a team.

Robin gives me the 15,000 Yemeni rials he still has on him. I haven't a clue how much that is, but it turns out to be about £80. I leave the guys for the time being and go outside to get a taxi to the Sheraton. The street is very noisy, with car horns blaring, and there is a posse of taxi drivers desperate for my fare. It takes about ten minutes to get to the Sheraton along crowded shopping streets. I meet Gamon, a tall, thin and bespectacled figure. Hassan, his colleague from the BBC *Arabic Service*, is a rugged, middle-aged Egyptian. They take me to a restaurant to meet the *World Service* team. They are polite but I sense there may be some hostility under the surface. My team has caused them a lot of headaches, however inadvertently.

I receive a very frank briefing on Bush House's priorities and local Yemeni politics. During these intense conversations, Hassan takes a call on his mobile. It is his government minders, saying that other government officials watching me have lost me at my hotel and are wondering where I have gone. He reassures them I am behaving myself, though he tells me they believe that I am working for the British Foreign Office. Hassan's mobile proves to be invaluable as the crisis unfolds, though we are not sure how safe it is to talk freely on it. A while ago, the Yemeni government closed the entire mobile network for a few months so they could install some sophisticated monitoring devices.

I go back to the Taj Sheba Hotel at about 10.30am and in the reception meet the boys again, who are now with their lawyer, Sheikh Tariq Abdullah. He is a cultured, intelligent, and precise man. He is very smartly dressed and sports a manicured grey beard. Sheikh Tariq is from Aden in south Yemen and has been honorary legal counsel to the British Embassy for 25 years.

While I am trying to weigh him up, the British Ambassador, Vic Henderson, arrives. We have a brief chat about tactics before setting off for the court house, where the team members are due for their daily questioning session. As we travel, I ask the Ambassador for a geo-political briefing, information about the kidnappings of foreigners and his thoughts on how we can find a solution to this current crisis with the three guys.

The court house is in a rundown complex with dozens of people milling around. We are taken through what is referred to as the 'court house garden'. This is a something of a misnomer, as there is hardly any grass; instead, there are some scruffy scrub bushes, and some empty cans. There is nothing to lift the spirits here. On the benches round the sides of the garden are groups of local stragglers and supplicants, anxious to plead for justice.

We are then led to the anteroom of the office of the District Attorney for Sana'a – number two to the Attorney General, or AG, as we come to call him. There are a few soldiers around dressed in bright fatigues and carrying machine guns. They do not seem to be that threatening and, indeed, shake our hands with apparent warmth. Some small-fry officials are seated behind a cracked and shoddy desk. We are swept into the next office where there are another ten people wandering around. I am introduced to a big man with fat, puffy cheeks, brown teeth and receding black hair. He is dressed in a truly awful safari suit. He beckons me and the British Ambassador to go upstairs with him. The three guys are asked to stay downstairs with their lawyer for yet more questioning.

As we go along a dingy corridor, the Ambassador tells me that our companion in the terrible safari suit is none other than the Attorney General himself, whom he hadn't met before. We are then ushered in through yet another anteroom, where there are a couple of other soldiers who look much more belligerent. The inner sanctum is large with a few grubby black sofas and chairs. Behind a large desk in one corner is an array of fax machines and phones, which keep going off, making an infuriating racket.

The AG asks me to sit next to him; the Ambassador sits opposite. The AG then proceeds to deliver what can only be described as a total dressing down. His English is reasonable, learnt when he went to school in Aden while it was under British rule. He is anxious to point out that he relished his part in helping to expel the British. Acting like a pantomime villain, he accuses our team of a whole host of misdemeanours, including the preposterous claim that Rageh has apparently admitted on the rushes of the team's filming trip to Bani Dhabyan that the BBC is part of British intelligence.

Throughout this tirade, he keeps clutching and caressing my arm and grinning manically, his eyes revolving all around the room. I wonder to myself whether the qat chew has started early today. He also attacks the Ambassador and complains to him about the behaviour of his number two, David Pearce. They have apparently had a stand-off when the AG was questioning the team shortly after their arrest. He calls the Ambassador a spy and accuses me of working for British intelligence as well. All in all a totally charming performance – and this from a man who is charged with upholding the rule of law in Yemen! He clearly is a very nasty piece of work and I shudder when I look at his dead, soulless eyes.

The AG's diatribe continues for many minutes. He also accuses the Embassy of smuggling cassette tapes for our team. The Ambassador hotly denies all this and I try several times to get a word in edgeways, but despite the screeching of the fax machine, the AG is determined to press home his points. A truce is finally called when one of the AG's underlings brings in a tray of refreshments – hot drinks and a bottle of thick mango juice, which you can only drink by slurping noisily. I don't think the AG would be a man bothered by such a lack of drinking manners.

After this altercation, the Ambassador drops me off back at the hotel. The hopes of an early solution are fast receding, given the AG's histrionics. I manage to snatch a bit of rest and make a few calls to London. The boys get back at 5.30pm from a lengthy and exhausting day of questioning. I immediately take them by the pool for a chat. They tell me the full details of their initial arrest and questioning, how they were picked up at a checkpoint by more than 50 threatening soldiers and taken to the Interior Ministry. They describe how they had locked themselves into the vehicle that had been transporting them around and refused to come out. Tense negotiations followed and they had an angry encounter with our friend the AG, who was carrying a pistol in the waistband of his atrocious safari suit. They tell me of the stress caused by their repeated questioning and sleep deprivation, both at the Ministry and then at the court house. They did not eat because the food looked horrible and there were only very basic toilet facilities.

All this went on for more than 50 hours. I listen intently as the tale unfolds; I haven't realised quite how frightening this period must have been.

Later, in a surreal development, I go with the boys to a somewhat incongruous Peruvian evening in one of the hotel's entertainment rooms. They might be under house arrest, but they can still buy tickets to this so-called entertainment. This is no time to relax, however; the table where we are asked to sit is by the door and alongside a wall next to another room. Co-incidence? Everything seems so normal, but are we under surveillance? The trouble with this hall of mirrors is that you can begin to imagine anything and you periodically feel foolish or rightly paranoid.

By now, I am feeling exhausted and I worry about being caught off-guard. The star turn of the evening, a Peruvian band, begins its routine. It is bizarre drifting into semi-consciousness, listening to the breathy pipes of the Andes. Am I exaggerating the severity of this crisis? After all, what is there to worry about? The great and good of Sana'a are gathered in their glad-rags. We are partaking of an exquisite bottle of Rioja in a country where alcohol is supposed to be banned. We are also noshing on an appetising array of food, from spicy chicken to mozzarella salad to blueberry mousse.

I find it hard to cope much longer and drag myself to bed, hoping that a little rest will restore my equilibrium. I am determined to sleep and manage to drop off for a couple of hours. Then I wake in a flash, realising that we are up against a formidable enemy in the belligerent AG and his superiors. I ring Fiona in the UK to warn her not to underestimate our hosts. I speak in such a jumbled rush that she must think I am barmy.

THURSDAY 4 JUNE

Unfortunately, the muse of sleep does not descend. I climb back into bed with my mind racing. Despite my weariness and pre-occupations, I still cling to my determination to get the guys out. I wish I hadn't had a couple of glasses of wine the night before, thereby breaking my rule about having no alcohol at a time of major crisis.

Soon, daylight arrives and we can begin the day with a trip to the hotel pool. It really is a lifesaver for Robin, Frank and Rageh – a way of trying to relax and work off the rich hotel food. We regard the pool as being safe from eavesdropping, so we can mutter numerous secrets as we criss-cross it. I try to engender a fighting spirit.

Afterwards, they have to leave for their routine questioning sessions but I decide to stay and make some more calls to London. When I eventually pitch up at the court house, I stumble by chance into a room where Robin is with our lawyer, Sheikh Tariq, and is being questioned by the chief prosecutor. I am again taken to the AG's office upstairs. Rageh and Frank are in there, drumming their fingers. So are James – from the British Embassy – and

Hassan, trying to weave his web on our behalf. The AG is closeted in a corner of the room with his deputy, the District Attorney. Apparently, he has found more cassette tapes to use as intimidating evidence and his focus is on them and not us.

Eventually, we entice the AG into a conversation. I suggest to him that the BBC will apply great pressure if the matter doesn't end quickly. In reply, he expresses his concern about what he regards as specific misdemeanours. He is again obsessed with Rageh's alleged confession that the BBC is a nest of spies. He is also now deeply suspicious of Robin, because on one tape he had corrected someone for pronouncing Bani Dhabyan wrongly. Robin had spoken with such confidence that the AG thinks Robin must be fluent in Arabic.

The AG then switches to the issue of qat. He says this will be the main attraction of the Arab weekend, which starts soon at lunch-time on Thursday. It looks like our hopes of obtaining a release before this are remote. In some ways, I am hoping he will invite us to an official qat chew so we can somehow turn that to our advantage. I am prepared to try anything to get the guys home.

Meanwhile, the AG continues with a paean of praise about the positive properties of qat. He says it makes him mentally alert and enables him to work on government papers until 3pm. Perhaps British cabinet ministers should learn from their Yemeni counterparts and chew some of this leaf to help them plough through their red boxes.

We just have to sit and humour the AG at this stage. We dare not provoke him until we know more about what is happening and why. After an hour or so, Rageh is summoned to another office for questioning. A few minutes later, Hassan and I are asked to go, too. We are allowed to have a quick spin through the cassette tapes which the Yemeni authorities say prove the guilt of our team. The footage seems pretty innocuous, with many shots of craggy mountain passes. The group of Yemeni law enforcement high-ups watching with us seem to be treating the whole matter as a game and start laughing and joking.

Then we find the key moment where Rageh allegedly incriminates himself. It is nonsense really. It is true that a tribal leader asks Rageh in Arabic whether the BBC is part of British intelligence and at first sight Rageh appears to agree that it is. However, Rageh doesn't understand Arabic and has simply given grunting assent to the leader in the sense of please go on, continue. It is a ridiculous, trumped-up charge. We in turn start laughing and joking and hope we can just shrug off this accusation of Rageh being a spy. It seems to have worked, at least for the time being.

Afterwards, I am allowed to ring Fiona from the AG's office and, mindful that others are probably listening, I give her a careful and polite summary of events so far. "It's all rubbish," concludes Fiona. "That's your view," I say mildly, desperate not to go on the attack until we know what charges will be brought, if any. I am aware that the AG is certainly not a bull to provoke.

After a few minutes, it is all over for the day. We hear the news that our team is to be charged but it is all pretty chaotic. It is hard to follow what exactly is happening. We become hopeful that we have indeed seen off the spying charges. Instead, the three guys face a relatively minor charge based on Sections 29 and 30 of Yemeni Press Law, which nobody has seen. At least we now know where we stand. We seem to have headed off the worst and there is no mention of the vitriolic allegations made yesterday by the AG against both the Embassy and the BBC. I think maybe I can take a much more open and critical stance now. Perhaps we can get even these charges dismissed and be home in the next two days – but deep down, I am still very disturbed. Hassan too is subdued; this is not what he was expecting. He thought there would be a very positive outcome with no charges.

Back at the hotel, our lawyer Sheikh Tariq drops a bombshell. We are all sitting for lunch together but he suggests that he and I should move to eat separately at a table in the corner. Between mouthfuls of fresh tomato soup, he calmly announces that there will definitely be a trial. I am shaken to the core. The situation is spinning out of control. How does he know? He cannot reveal how he does and says I cannot identify him as a source either, so I have to keep this news quiet from Robin, Frank and Rageth. I have been put in a terrible position. Sheikh Tariq tells me that he is certain the trial will begin on Saturday, the day I am hoping we can go home. My mind begins to race. I have to urge the office in London to put more pressure on the Yemeni government. I also have to somehow communicate to the team that the situation remains serious without compromising Sheikh Tariq.

When I return to their table, the boys try to pump me for information. I will have to keep some things secret to protect them, I say.

I rush up to my room to call London and ask Fiona to go round to the office of Mark Damazer, Head of BBC Current Affairs, so I can speak to them both together on a speaker phone at their end. I call them back in a couple of minutes and explain that the situation is very, very serious. I can't give the full picture because we are on an open line. Despite the constraints of my visa, I am desperate to send a signal that it is now time to get tough and apply as much pressure as possible. The main purpose of the call is to say that the key to any solution is now political. The legal case is something of a sideshow. There is certainly no case for the team to answer – and I am determined to be very robust about that, even on an open line. I know I have to shake the senior bosses out of their complacency, however understandable that is. Fiona of course has been on the warpath virtually since day one, but in the midst of other frenetic activity in the broadcasting world, it is sometimes hard to attract the full attention of senior executives.

Fiona intimates that she is going to attend an award ceremony for the One World Broadcasting Trust and is going to try to collar there the newly-appointed Secretary of State for International Development, Clare Short, whom she knows from her days as a political correspondent at *Channel Four News*. Aid, Fiona declares boldly, is clearly very important to Yemen and perhaps something can be done to apply some pressure.

It does cross my mind too that maybe I could also be implicated in the crisis and be taken in for questioning. For the first time, I feel a chink appear in my stance of determination and cold, measured anger. Fear is beginning to creep in. I have to keep my nerve and think clearly.

While London bosses are chewing over what to do next, I proceed with establishing the terms of the legal case against our team. Sheikh Tariq tells me that although the charges are minor, there is a risk of a prison sentence. He thinks a fine will be the more likely outcome but the possibility of a one-year jail sentence cannot be ruled out. I decide at this stage to keep that information from the boys, who have understandably retreated to their rooms to lie on their beds and gather their thoughts. I ask the lawyer point blank: will they be convicted? He says he thinks it is probable.

The crisis now gathers pace. The Ambassador and his colleague, James, call round to see me and we share a coffee together in the tea-room. They are in a bullish and supportive mood. The ambassador says he will contact the Yemeni Prime Minister to see what he can do.

James points out the irony of the situation; the only people who have been charged are those who have done nothing wrong. The tribal kidnappers are still free, despite the authorities knowing who they are. I raise another irony: the Interior Ministry's case is that our three guys were told for their own protection that they should not go to the tribal areas. In the event, though, the team remained perfectly safe until they returned to the capital, where they effectively had been kidnapped by the government and placed under house arrest. Even though the team members are staying in a posh hotel, they are still not free to leave.

The Ambassador tells me more about the power struggles in the Yemeni body politic; the hard-liners basically are in the Interior and Information Ministries. They are manipulating this case to suit their own ends and put pressure on the prime minister. Another theory doing the rounds is that the president is being lobbied by his maternal uncle, who favours Yemen pumping up its traditional anti-western stance.

I rush back upstairs after a while to have a big conference call with London. This time, it is also attended by the Chief Executive of BBC News, Tony Hall, and his deputy, Richard Ayre. It has been amazing to gather these bosses together on a day when, as bad luck would have it, strikes have been taking place at the BBC. I am frustrated, as I have to remain calm and not say anything rash or foolish that can be seized on by the eavesdropping Yemeni authorities. Again I urge an escalation of pressure and to meet a political situation with a strong political response.

One missing link in all this is Hassan, who is out and about ferreting out snippets of information. His contacts are mainly with the Yemeni security people, who openly follow him around, and with the hard-line Information Ministry. He may well have other sources, of course, but he is hearing a lot from people with a line to peddle. The hard-liners are keen to deflect any frontal attack on their position, so very cleverly will invent false deadlines to weaken the resolve of their opponents. By now, Hassan is becoming furious; he feels betrayed, as he never expected charges to be brought.

We agree that we need a council of war with our lawyer. I know I have to weigh up the sometimes conflicting advice given by Sheikh Tariq and Hassan. It is good to get out of the hotel to go to Sheikh Tariq's house, which is near some Western embassies. We sit around on low-level seats, thrashing out the problem. We first pore over the country's media regulations and believe we have a strong defence case.

I wonder whether we can offer an olive branch. What about making something known in the trade as a 'non-apology apology'? Something along the lines of: "The BBC expresses regret if there has been any offence caused," but without directly apologising for any of the BBC's actions. I am anxious to come up with something that will avoid a trial, though Hassan feels it will be showing too much weakness at this stage to offer up such a statement. I say that the three guys need to relax a little tomorrow after such a destabilising and draining day today. It seems that, under the conditions of their house arrest, we can leave the hotel on a short trip, provided their security minders escort us.

When I get back to the hotel, I suggest a morale-boosting trip of sight-seeing. We have a meal together but the mood is sombre and downbeat. It is then up to my room to make the final call of the day. I talk to Mark Damazer and he says momentum is building in London. We agree a little pressure has been taken off for the time being, as we all seem to think Friday – a holiday – will be quiet. We could not be more wrong.

FRIDAY 5 JUNE

I manage six hours of sleep – a triumph, given the circumstances. On waking, I make a couple of calls – one to home and another to Mark. During these conversations, I stress how angry I am. I am not sure whether it will do any good, but I think it is important to show the authorities some strength and spirit. I flick on the television and just happen to catch a package on *BBC World* about the arrests of the BBC team in Yemen. It is by Brian Hanrahan, who came to fame during the Falklands War. The report is brief and contains pictures of Rageh, with an interview clip with Mark Damazer in which he appeals for the release of the team. It is something of a boost to morale but in my bones I wish that more fuss was being made. The day begins lazily with our swim. The guys are a bit more relaxed outwardly, but keep dropping in gallows humour jokes about going to prison.

During breakfast I take a call from Fiona. She sounds on good form and tells me in coded language about some plans she is hatching. She is pulling every string that is dangling. Four years earlier, *Assignment* ran a film about Hillary Clinton, and Fiona apparently intends to exploit some contact she made with the First Lady's staff. I am convinced there are two main lines of attack we can use in any PR battle; one is about image – the continued detention of the three is going down badly in the West and is helping to portray Yemen as anti-Western and anti-democratic. However, I am disturbed to think that there might be some factions in Yemen that are happy to project this image. The Interior Ministry, for one, is probably delighted, so I think there might be more mileage in the second strategy – this concerns money, business, trade, and aid. A dilution of Western economic support will hurt everyone in Yemen, including the hard-liners. Fiona agrees this is a better tack to pursue. She also warns me elliptically about the power and reach of the security forces.

The guys and I then decide to go on an outing to the King's Palace, about twenty minutes away from Sana'a. Suddenly I feel in an upbeat mood. Seeing Frank waiting in reception, I mutter to him with a swagger: "We are going to beat these bastards." Our taxi is followed by a four-wheel drive vehicle laden with security officers. On the way, we stop at a dusty clearing to look across a steep valley with stupendous views. Under different circumstances, it would be exhilarating. On the drive, we each chat about our journalistic adventures. This is the first time anyone in the team has been arrested. I say that although I have worked in many countries, they are ahead of me on that one; I have never been arrested – well, not yet.

At the palace there is chance to speak more freely out of earshot of the taxi driver, who can speak English. Is this a co-incidence? Probably not. I warn the three guys what we might be up against – that there is a strong possibility that the security services are much more organised than we might expect in such a seemingly ramshackle, chaotic country. We wander in and out of small rooms at the palace and at one stage I climb into what appears to be a tiny prison cell. I shudder inwardly; it is a bit too near the knuckle. The three filmed here at the start of their trip; it was carefree and exciting then, but not anymore. I can tell it is dawning on them that they may be in this for the long haul.

On the way back, we stop on top of a hill overlooking Sana'a, which lies in a huge bowl, full of mystery and medieval resonance. We point out some gravestones near the rudimentary car-park and ask what they are. The bodies of Chinese workers, killed while building the road, comes the reply. We clamber back into the taxi, deep in thought. During the journey, the driver shows a keen interest in whether negotiations over re-establishing a direct British Airways flight to Yemen will be successful. I take this as a sign that that this could be another opportunity in our possible attempt to exert some commercial pressure. I make a mental note to pass this on to Fiona to investigate.

Back at the hotel, we quickly settle into our established routine and eat a comforting, huge buffet lunch. But it is not so soothing today, as we have to listen to the strains of a Polish musical duo. Their disharmonies tug away at the psyche. Discord and uncertainty are too disturbing, so we concentrate on tucking into the food – huge platefuls of prawns, chips, salads and sticky puddings. We are all by now addicted to fresh strawberry juice and order it by the tray load. Although it is a de facto prison, the staff members at the hotel are very attentive and understanding. They always know where we are and a member of staff will trot up to us quickly with a mobile phone in hand if a call comes through.

The guys have taken to soothing their nerves by smoking copiously. Whenever they reach for a cigarette, one of the waiters clad in red jackets will rush up and push a lighter under their noses. What a weird place this is. It is like being in a gilded cage; luxury food and plush surroundings, waiters who are eager to please. At the same time, there remains a gnawing sensation in your gut that the team can be called any time for more interrogation and, of course, the threat of prison is becoming ever closer.

While we are finishing lunch, our lawyer unexpectedly arrives. As if to confirm our insecurities, he delivers another bombshell. He doesn't beat about the bush and simply informs us that a trial will go ahead and will begin at 10am tomorrow.

CHAPTER SIX

Rescue Mission in Yemen: The Trial

I can see the boys wilt and their shoulders droop in response to the unwelcome news that there will be a trial. There is an excruciating silence while everyone tries to digest the information. Even I, who have been told the trial will proceed, am momentarily nonplussed. I suppose I have been hoping for something to avoid this madness. I say I think the team needs time to reflect on this and I rush back to my room to inform London. It is hard to get through, but eventually I track down Fiona. Are you sure it is a full trial, she asks? Our Bush colleagues apparently are still briefing London that the situation might not be that serious. I imagine the advice that may be being passed on: hold off; keep calm; wait and see; take no risks. They are the supine mantras of the Foreign Office and their acolytes down the generations – far better, old boy, to sort this out over a whisky in the library.

But this wait-and-see approach isn't working. I say I will double-check about the status of the trial but suggest that a press statement can be made along the following bald lines: "The trial of the BBC team in Yemen is scheduled to open at 10am tomorrow in a court in Sana'a, according to the defence lawyer working for the BBC."

I return downstairs to talk to Sheikh Tariq and our team. He says we all have a lot of work to do that afternoon preparing for the trial. He has been to see the District Attorney, the AG's deputy, and has seen the actual charge sheet. There are one or two extra offences mentioned and the penal code charges have seemingly been stiffened. It is scary news and again events seem to be spiralling out of control. The guys look dejected and demoralised. One moment they were hoping to recover from a big lunch by having a gentle snooze in their rooms; now they are being asked to roll up their sleeves and prepare to defend themselves in a court of law in a strange and unpredictable land. I call Hassan and he rushes around. "I can't believe it," he wails. "I have been betrayed. These guys could go to prison! What is happening?"

We leave for Sheikh Tariq's house to work in peace and quiet. I am now much more jittery, especially given Fiona's stark warning about the security services. My mood is made worse when we pass a huge, modern building in the centre of the city. "What is that?" I inquire innocently. "Internal Security Headquarters," comes the reply from Sheikh Tariq. When we arrive at the house, I am not convinced it will be totally safe to talk openly. He, though, is confident. "No-one can get in," he says. "Besides, I have a man who looks after the house."

"Is he here today?" I ask nervously.

"No, it's his day off."

This reply doesn't do much for my sang-froid. I can't believe that Sheikh Tariq is not a possible target for surveillance. However, I decide that I must calm down. This is probably the best place we have to retreat to and we just have to get on with our full and frank preparations. Hassan also tells me I am inflating the abilities of the secret police. By now, though, it is very difficult to trust anyone. I have received much advice and many opinions. The only person who has told me anything that *has* actually happened is Sheikh Tariq.

The afternoon session turns out to be draining. London keeps ringing up to see what we are planning. I suppose I should be grateful that the bosses are now really taking matters seriously. The British Ambassador also rings up for a briefing. Time is slipping by, as the London bosses have an important get-together at 4.30pm our time. As we thrash everything out, I am conscious that what really matters is the view of the three guys. They are the ones in the eyes of the storm; it is they who risk going to prison. This is no mere strategic-thinking exercise; any wrong move could jeopardise the well-being of my three colleagues. We come up with a three-point plan: the BBC in London must be bolder and step up its pressure; we will push a version of the non-apology apology option; and Sheikh Tariq says he has a few tricks up his sleeve and will ask for the case to be thrown out immediately when the trial starts because the evidence is poor.

The boys are happy to go along with the non-apology apology, provided there is no hint of guilt or wrong-doing on their part. They are also anxious to emphasise the word 'misunderstanding'. We want to keep Sheikh Tariq's tricks from the authorities, who are undoubtedly monitoring the line, and so we have to devise a coded form of words to communicate his strategy. I come up with a simple sentence: *Michael Mansfield* (a well-known human rights lawyer in the UK, but code for our lawyer) *will do a Paul Daniels* (i.e. rabbit out of the hat) *on the day the Blind Date programme goes out* (i.e. Saturday – tomorrow). They get the message but are desperate to know more about the rabbit. We can't let on, as that will defeat the object.

I run the guys through what I propose to say in a follow-up call to Mark Damazer. The phone call starts off well, although there is a lot of tension in the air. Mark probes more about the strategy to go for an escalation of pressure. He starts to use a coded cricketing analogy, so I say it is like a limited overs game. We are behind the run rate and need to step up our scoring.

I finish my party piece and then hand the phone to Hassan. He says it would be better to hold off any big pressure today, and then go for a full escalation in 48 hours if no release has occurred. The boys and I stare at each other in consternation. What on earth is he doing? We wanted firm action now, tonight. Why hasn't he told us this is what he is going to say?

I can sit still no longer. I snatch the phone from Hassan just twenty seconds into his contribution. I try to carry out some damage limitation but it is all a mess. The boys slump back in their seats in stunned silence. The tension becomes even more unbearable. However, I cannot risk too much of an almighty stand-up row. I know I still need Hassan as an ally. Perhaps there is some logic in his actions, though he should still have argued his case with us first.

Around 9pm, we break up for the evening. It has been a long day – so much for the hopes of grabbing a rest to revitalise bruised spirits! There is even worse to come; when we arrived back at the Taj Sheba Hotel, Hassan draws me to one side. We go for a wander along the pavement, talking in low voices. I am astounded by the tone of his comments. He tells me never to humiliate him again by grabbing the phone off him in front of everyone. He is so offended that he says he is seriously thinking of leaving Yemen tomorrow and abandoning us to our own fates. I am startled. I apologise for any offence caused (another non-apology apology!), but explain that he sprang a nasty surprise on us. The boys have been clearly shocked by his advice to tone down any talk of escalating the pressure. I also plead with Hassan not to leave – we need him.

After several more moments of tense exchanges, he calms down a little, but then goes on to accuse me of being a James Bond figure. He asks me why I am talking so much in code with London. I reply that I have been playing it safe because I don't know how much I can get away with on the phone and I would be grateful if he has any advice for me on that score. I say that now the trial is definite, I will be quite happy to be virtually fully on the record the whole time. Confusingly, he then says I should not abandon all coded conversations, but suggests I give them something of a rest for a while. I wander back into the hotel on my own, completely bewildered and demoralised. It hits me even more graphically that I am in a strange country and culture – and do not possess the mechanisms to deal with it.

I discover that the team have drifted into what has come naturally to them after more than a week at the hotel – eating a big meal in the restaurant. As I am clearing my plate, I am handed the phone by one of the attentive members of staff. It is the British Ambassador on the line. His manner is breathless; "I've just spoken to Iriyani," (the Yemeni Prime Minister) he says. "He has made an offer. If your team pleads guilty at the hearing tomorrow, they will receive a minor punishment and will be allowed to leave the country on Sunday night." I thank him and immediately pass on the offer to the guys. Once again, their nerves are jangling – just when they are contemplating getting some rest in order to psyche themselves up for the forthcoming trial.

I say I should immediately phone London. I leave the team to think more about the offer, which on the face of it is deeply unattractive. They have done nothing wrong, so pleading guilty will stick in their craw. They are also deeply suspicious about whether the Yemenis will stick to their word. I again race into the lift on the way to my room, my heart pounding. I call Mark Damazer, who immediately says he will check with the Foreign Office in London for its advice. He asks me to push the Ambassador on whether there will be any definite guarantees. I also decide to call Sheikh Tariq, whose view is as lucid as always. He believes the offer is worrying as it is very tough, and should be rejected.

I go back to talk to Robin, Frank and Rageh and ask them to gather for a pow-wow in Robin's room. I take down a few mini Mars bars I brought with me from home to lift morale. If the cabinet can have their qat chew, we can have our Mars bar chew. I am very anxious that the security men don't hear this conversation, so we turn up the television loud and squat on the bed, whispering to each other. By co-incidence, *BBC World* is showing a *Correspondent* film on Kosovo, reported by our colleague Phil Rees, one of the programme's most experienced cloak-and-dagger merchants. We chuckle to ourselves, thinking how much he would enjoy this bizarre situation. But the levity does not last long; we all know this is an extremely serious moment, perhaps decisive.

I go through the offer again and pass on the views of Sheikh Tariq. I say that if there are no guarantees, it is not even worth discussing. The three listen intently as I stress that I cannot tell them which way to go. It is entirely a matter for them and their own personal consciences. It is them in the dock and not me. I ask each of them in turn for their decision; all are in unison. They refuse to be cowed and say they will not go home with their tails between their legs. We now assume that the trial will definitely go ahead, though with an uncertain ending. One thing for sure is that the team will definitely enter 'not guilty' pleas.

As I wander back to my room, the full gravity of the situation presses down on me. I admire the fortitude and bravery of the guys and but feel very depressed and scared. This is the worst hour of the crisis for me up until now, though obviously the team has suffered much worse traumas during the 50 hours of questioning when they were first detained. My imagination begins to run away with me – where will it end? Will I be arrested as well, even attacked? I even wonder whether I might be bumped off – highly fanciful, I know, but such is my mood. If I am having such thoughts, how are Robin, Frank, and Rageh feeling? The nightly ceremony of putting the chain of the door of my room is carried out with even more care tonight.

Before bed, there is time for one last call from Mark. He has had word from the Ambassador that there are no guarantees and the British Foreign Office has said it could do nothing if the team pleads guilty and then is sent to prison. Gamon has also told him this is a disturbing offer and he cannot work out what is going on. I tell Mark we have already decided to reject the offer and are going ahead with the trial.

SATURDAY 6 JUNE

I have been hoping for a long sleep, but after such a haunting few hours, there is no chance. First I have to deal with an uncontrollable outbreak of fear, which happily soon evaporates. I am surprising myself by remaining so focused and determined. I do not know where this strength is coming from, apart from a heightened sense of outrage and an unwavering commitment to get the team out.

I ring Mark and we discuss some options for how the day might pan out. I stress how brave the team has been and urge that anyone doubting their journalistic nous should be sat upon immediately. I then ring the Ambassador at his residence and ask him whether he is coming to the court hearing. "Oh no," he exclaims. "I have to take the dog to the vet. It has an abscess on its bottom and needs attention. After that I'll be going shopping with the wife."

It is comforting to know that Her Majesty's finest is on the case! He does say he will be sending his deputy James in his place, so at least he hasn't checked out completely.

The three guys behave almost like condemned men, though they also have an air of resolution and determination. Meanwhile, a fashion crisis is developing – what to wear in court. Frank is agonising because he has no jacket and is unsure whether that matters. Rageh doesn't have a tie on him and can't work out whether it will be sacrilege to enter court without one. I cut through these Gordian knots extremely quickly. Here are two easy decisions to make for a change! I tell Frank to buy a jacket and put it down on expenses. In fact, it will be an amusing claim – purchase of jacket to attend important court hearing. Rageh does the same. Neither comes cheap as they are Western-imported goods, but I believe it will be money well spent if it shows the judge that they are smart, serious professionals. One major problem they continually face in an Arab society such as this is their youth. Anything they can do to offset their lack of years will be a great advantage. It was a bit easier for me to play the big BBC boss, being at least a decade older, with accompanying grey hairs.

While we are waiting in the hotel reception, there is another moment of mind-boggling weirdness. The piped music system is playing *Please Release Me*. Is it a sick joke being played by the secret police? Or a message of support from our loyal hotel staff? No, that is taking conspiracy theories too far, and I tell myself to remain calm. Still, it's a strange co-incidence nonetheless.

We set off for the courthouse in convoy. Our lawyer, Sheikh Tariq, also looks determined, resplendent in a smart suit. He gives us all confidence as we progress through the rubbish-strewn streets. Typically, the day does not unfold as we expect. Instead of being ushered into court, we are asked to wait outside the District Attorney's office. It is hot and there are groups of supplicants waiting for a glimpse of the AG. Hassan is with us and he is mobbed by the crowd. His informed and colourful reports on the *BBC Arabic Service* have made him something of a local cult figure. I ask James from the British Embassy the burning question of the day. How is the Ambassador's dog?

After half an hour, we are summoned into the District Attorney's office. It looks like horse trading is first on the agenda – politics before the formal legal process. I hardly get through the door before I am set upon by the AG and a couple of others. I realised I am being hustled into making a hasty decision. They say the guys can now enter a 'not guilty' plea here and now if they want to, outside the courtroom. They will receive a minor sentence but will immediately be sent home. It looks like the AG is uncertain how well his case will go in a full court room when it comes under public scrutiny, so he wants to do a squalid behind-the-scenes deal.

Hassan is by my side, urging me to seize this opportunity to settle quickly, but an inner voice urges caution. I remember that when someone has a weak case they can sometimes go on the attack to try to hide their poor hand, so I manage to grab a word with Sheikh Tariq. "We have time," he says. "They seem to be moving; let's wait." I am mightily cheered up. We have shown strength the night before and there has been a response. If we hold the line now, there might be more movement – and indeed there is. We discover the charges have already been reduced and this means that the court will have less flexibility to impose a prison term. However, a suspended sentence is much more of a possibility.

We are now into serious horse-trading. Hassan, Sheikh Tariq, the three guys and I all sit at one end of the room in a huddle. All the legal officials say that the President wants a resolution by the end of the day – so do we. Perhaps we can turn this momentum to our advantage. I remember that James from the Embassy has given me a copy of a letter the Ambassador has written by hand to Prime Minister Iriyani. It is based on the non-apology apology formula we discussed before. The Ambassador was going to mention this formula when he spoke to Iriyani last night but was outflanked when Iriyani dropped the bombshell of the pleading guilty offer.

The three guys are happy with the Ambassador's letter. It gives nothing away but is a meaty goodwill gesture. I can now forgive the Ambassador for appearing to put the fate of his dog's bottom ahead of our team; perhaps his hand-written letter can be the key which unlocks the negotiations.

Sheikh Tariq wants to fight on with great vigour; Hassan is urging caution. Frank asks me what I think. I say we have to work out our bottom line and aim to escape as quickly as we can. My view is that the trial should be open and they should be allowed to enter their plea of 'not guilty'. It is important to do this in public and not agree to the AG's proposed shoddy, furtive deal. We have also to try to ensure that there will only be a derisory fine.

Everyone agrees they can live with this. So off we go — the three of us, Hassan, Sheikh Tariq, and me, to chew the cud with the Attorney General and his deputy. They move remarkably quickly and say they want the trial to go ahead. They point out that they are now filing lesser charges and will ask only for a medium penalty and not the highest one. We ask what this means — we receive no satisfactory answer, as the AG does not rule out a suspended sentence. In any case, I ask how we can trust them to keep their side of the bargain. Our lawyer stresses we can believe the AG's word.

I am obviously not convinced, but realise it will be provocative — and possibly dangerous — to express further doubt. It will be tantamount to calling him a liar. Later, Sheikh Tariq tells me that the AG had visibly been shaken by even my initial inquiry. He was able to calm him down by saying what I really meant was, 'how could I persuade the team that the offer was genuine?'. God bless Sheikh Tariq.

I withdraw for another pow-wow. Sheikh Tariq thinks we still seem to be getting somewhere and we should press for more concessions. Hassan takes the opposite view. It is like bareback riding, I think to myself.

By now, it is 11.30am and the trial has still not begun. Of course, political considerations are paramount here and it's not the time for scruples. I try to remain cool, but again am well aware that any wrong decision can harm the lives of three people.

I decide to have one final huddle with the three guys. Frank is quite rightly very unhappy with any possibility of a suspended sentence. He says he will have to declare this when travelling to somewhere like the United States and it could lead to all sorts of complications. In addition, it would still imply they were guilty and could also have a detrimental impact for BBC journalists operating in other parts of the Arab world. Rageh is equally vehement, so I become emboldened once again. The AG seems to be moving, so I decide to play it tough, take a bit of poetic licence and tell a little porkie.

"London won't wear a suspended sentence," I say. The AG looks peeved. I ask him whether there is any chance he could rule it out.

"I cannot influence the judge," he mutters darkly. Oh yeah, I say to myself. But quick as a flash, the AG does say that if the judge doesn't impose a suspended sentence, he will not appeal against the decision. He also says we can appeal if we feel the sentence is too harsh. Apart from that, he can go no further. He says in Arabic to Hassan that I would do well to heed an Arab proverb, 'You cannot leech the market', presumably meaning that I should not push my luck. I am frustrated – so near and yet so far.

I also press the AG about the film rushes that the team shot during their trip to the tribal areas. He says flatly that they will not be handed back and he will ask for a court order to destroy them. We eventually all shuffle into the court room, which is calm and quiet. After a few moments, several groups of people pour in, including about ten Arab journalists. The authorities are undecided whether to place our team in the normal place for defendants, behind the bars of a Mafia-style cage.

Mercifully, Sheikh Tariq insists our team is placed on rickety chairs in front of the cage. Hassan is frantically working on an Arabic translation of our goodwill statement. Before he can finish, he is summoned to be the official court translator – then we have a big break.

When the judge appears, Sheikh Tariq turns to me and gleefully whispers, "Good news, they've given us a liberal judge."

I am delighted and dread to think what might have happened if the unseen forces we are facing would have succeeded in imposing a hard-line judge. The liberal judge before us is only in his thirties. He turns out to have a great sense of humour and spends most of the next hour smiling.

The judge laughs when the charges are read out. Some are clearly preposterous, including importing a satellite phone. The team members had obviously brought one in as part of their professional work. The judge also seems keen to discomfit the prosecutor, an excellent sign for us. My spirits rise. I cannot make head nor tail of the proceedings, as everyone is speaking so quietly. Hassan takes up station next to the three defendants. The only bit I really understand is when the three clearly and bravely state their 'not guilty' pleas. I suddenly notice that my legs are trembling. It must be the pent-up tension building up over the last few days.

It becomes clear that matters are after all not going to be concluded today. An adjournment is agreed until 8.30am the next morning. Hassan then motions for me to come with him and meet the judge in his private room. With him is the District Attorney, who throughout has been dressed in a Western-style jacket and tie. Hassan goes into overdrive to practise his black arts and the judge appears to warm to him. Afterwards, Hassan tells me that the judge has ruled out the possibility of a suspended sentence. So should we go for a deal now, he asks? In my view, no; the judge might be lying. He might change his mind overnight. He might have his mind changed for him. He might be changed for a more authoritarian judge.

As we leave the court room, I am ensnared by the AG, who is far too pally for my liking. It isn't long before he reverts to type.

He hisses aggressively into my ear, "Be careful of your lawyer. He wants to prolong these proceedings so he can make more money. He wants a big show trial. People like him don't really want to help their clients and some of them drag out their cases for up to a year."

I immediately recognise another negotiating trick. Within a minute, he turns nice again. He holds my arm and takes me for a walk round the by now very familiar unkempt garden at the court house. It is like being hugged by the devil himself. He stares at me. I stare back and refuse to be intimidated. It is clear that he is a bully and a coward. As we promenade à deux, he calls me a cold Englishman, a man of the mountains. The AG finishes our unpleasant groping session by announcing that I have been an honoured guest in Sana'a. If that is the case, I'd hate to see how he treats his enemies.

After more conversations, we leave. This is the best day I have had while in Sana'a, but again we keep our feet on the ground. Sheikh Tariq is determined to press home the momentum which seems to be shifting our way. He arranges for us to go over to his house again and do more preparatory work for tomorrow's proceedings. Everyone retires to their rooms for a while; I call Fiona, who remains sceptical, but I explain that there has been enough movement to call off any big publicity blitz until tomorrow. I also call the Ambassador to update him and he invites me over to the British Embassy. It is a huge compound and a welcome change of scene. I am very remiss and forget to ask about the dog's bottom.

When we arrive at Sheikh Tariq's house, we can hardly keep our eyes open. He, though, is indomitable. He puts the three guys through their paces; he asks them to consider how they will explain away the weaknesses in their case – how can they explain the fact that all their rooms in the hotel had *Do Not Disturb* signs on them when they slipped away secretly to the tribal area of Bani Dhabyan? It seems that the two security guards watching them had fallen asleep and did not notice them leaving.

It is very hard work but, back at the hotel, there is a welcome change of mood. The dining room has been given over to a Filipino band – two male musicians and three female vocalists dressed in fairly short skirts. How can they get away with this in conservative Sana'a? I have more calls to make, of course, but manage to get four hours sleep.

SUNDAY 7 JUNE

The big day dawns. Is today the day we escape this nightmare? We are all in the pool by 7.15am. The court hearing is set to start at 8.30am, though proceedings begin 30 minutes late. James from the Embassy is translating for me, so I understand much more. The prosecutor is hopeless and Sheikh Tariq demolishes most of his attack. The guys respond to specific allegations with confidence and assurance, and fortunately are not quizzed at all on the detail. My hopes rise. Sheikh Tariq launches into his concluding defence remarks, but then calamity strikes again – or so it seems. He and the prosecutor have a ferocious exchange which ends with Sheikh Tariq calling the team's female fixer as a witness. This is opening up a dangerous new front; he did not mention it to us the previous evening.

Everything descends into farce and proceedings are halted. During this hiatus, Hassan accosts me: "I will beat him up," he grunts furiously.

Hassan believes the lawyer's actions may jeopardise our case and worries that he is ostentatiously dragging the prime minister too much into the case. He is concerned that the prosecutor might call some local witnesses of his own in a tit-for-tat move and that might prolong things for weeks, if not months. I can see how this approach might drag us into a more overt power struggle between the prime minister, the president and his more authoritarian allies. I am also perplexed about why our lawyer has pulled this particular rabbit out of the hat without telling us. But he says he will stick only to the permission issue and not ask more political questions about the authority of the prime minister.

It is my call again. I can see that the AG doesn't want our fixer on the stand and know that when we remain strong, they crumble a bit – so put her on the stand, I say. But now the smiling judge hijacks events anyway. He asks her to sit right at the front of the court and then summarises her evidence for the recorder. In other words, he is fixing the final record of her testimony. No-one is allowed a cross-examination.

Amid all this tension and uncertainty, there is a supreme moment of humour. We see sudden movements behind the three defendants. Several dishevelled tribesmen begin to swarm into the Mafia-style cage, thinking it is time for their trial. No one has told them that our case is taking priority and they have turned up at the back entrance, anxious to have their day in court as soon as possible. They chat away volubly and heatedly. Bewildered expressions all round. A court clerk shoos them away; the judge thinks it is a hoot.

After all this melodrama, events come rapidly to a close. Sheikh Tariq makes an impassioned final oration and then Hassan reads out our goodwill statement. The judge grins at me. I begin to think the unthinkable for the first time. The judge adjourns the court and says he will be back in an hour to deliver his verdict. We stagger outside for some fresh air and I call Fiona. We are all excited.

The judge comes back in less than an hour. He rattles off his judgement in Arabic. Suddenly all around me people are putting up their thumbs and grinning at me. James says the judge is talking about the benefits of press freedom, which must be respected. Then the verdict: NOT GUILTY, and all the team's tapes to be returned to them. Spontaneous applause rings round the room. Some say it is the first time such scenes have occurred in a Yemeni court room. We all hug one another. There are several Arab journalists among the throng and they are clearly delighted. I am absolutely speechless. We have kept our nerve and have reaped our reward. Well done, Sheikh Tariq.

We rush out into the sunshine and call Fiona. Hassan is beside himself wanting to break the news so, in a spirit of reconciliation, I let him. Fiona too is thrilled but still cautious. We talk about booking flights for this evening and jump for joy. I ask Sheikh Tariq whether we should thank the judge. He says he has run off laughing down the road to avoid the AG and so prevent him lodging an appeal. Total victory seems to be ours! The AG himself looks totally dejected. He manages a limp handshake with me but cannot look any of us in the eye. Humiliating a bad guy always has a sweet fragrance. I learn later that the AG was especially angry with me because he felt I had gone back on a deal. This is not true; on the Saturday morning, we had concocted 95 per cent of a deal that would stick. We would have totally agreed not to go for a public trial if he had given us a guarantee about not imposing a suspended sentence – but he didn't, and I am immensely chuffed that he has the impression that I have double-crossed him. It couldn't have happened to a nicer man.

It is handshakes and backslapping all round outside the courtroom. After a few more minutes, we pile back in our four-wheel drive and go for a celebratory lunch at the hotel.

All the staff are pleased and the final buffet is even more special than usual. I am still trying to keep everybody's feet on the ground. It is never over until it's over, I warn, feeling like a terrible party-pooper. We all realise that this has been a bad defeat for the law enforcement agencies and they might get very nasty after being provoked. We have an appointment to pick up our tapes and equipment at the court house at 6.30pm. We have a final drink by the pool and all three of the team are having to pinch themselves. One moment the prospect of going to prison, the next minute the allure of London in flaming June, watching the World Cup with a cold beer.

I go to pack and think about having a final relaxing swim. As I head for the pool, I notice the door is open in the room next to mine. I see two men dressed in blue overalls inside. Both have what look like screwdrivers hanging down from their belts. One of them is taking out what appears to be electrical equipment from a cupboard near where the television is. Oh, they must be the phone-tappers and surveillance operatives, I think to myself in a remarkably blasé way. Such a thing all seems so normal here.

A left-field thought strikes me that perhaps they aren't from the secret police at all and are just television repair men. But come on – this is Yemen.

While in the pool, I reflect on the truly extraordinary experience of my mission. I am very grateful to the many people who have supported me back in the UK and here in Yemen. I calculate that I've had about 18 hours sleep in five days. Whatever else, it has been an incredible voyage operating in a city full of spies, informers, Sheikhs, bullies, ambassadors, machine-gun toting chewers of qat and bolshy tribesmen.

Overall, I reflect on the bravery of the BBC three; true musketeers all. They did not flinch when their journalistic commitment was put to the test. To me, this is worth more than a thousand comments in the press about the BBC's attachment to quality journalism.

So the time for reflection is over, and I turn my mind to practical matters. I want to see the hotel manager to try to get some money knocked off the bill. He is nowhere to be found. We also have some problems confirming the flights home but manage it in the end. A now rejuvenated Robin also tries optimistically to fix an interview with the prime minister but this proves difficult, so I say let's cut our losses. We need to pick up our equipment and leave. We depart on our own at 6pm for the court house. We feel vulnerable and unprotected without the oversight of our joint champions, Hassan and Sheikh Tariq.

The guys relive the bad times while under arrest, as well as the more positive ones. We are now well into qat chewing time and, as usual, it is very unnerving to see armed grown men with partly-chewed qat leaves stuffed into their cheeks like hamsters. It is even more disturbing to realise that many high-ups in the country try to conduct important business while semi-stoned. Soon everyone turns up at the court house – Hassan, our lawyer, and the district attorney. The equipment is returned to us, but then we receive another blow to the solar plexus; not all the tapes have been given back, especially the crucial ones shot in the tribal areas. The Interior Ministry still has them and no-one can be found who knows anything about them. The guys are anxious and extremely frustrated to be thwarted at the eleventh hour.

As time passes, I start to worry about our situation. I decide to leave early to pay the hotel bill. It is a nightmare; it takes about half an hour to print all the pages with the many room stays, lunches, phone calls etc. Then it takes another half hour to sort out the payment. I have to use US dollars, rials and my credit card. I continue to try to get some money off. Immoral earnings, I cry. I track down the hotel general manager, who says it is just business for them and they too have been inconvenienced. He says that when the team had first disappeared into the tribal areas, the security men had come to the hotel and threatened to turn it upside down. All the staff were closely questioned and intimidated.

"What a crazy place Yemen is," he says. He can say that again. Eventually, he says he will knock ten per cent off the phone bill.

"Not enough," I retort. But given that time is running out, we agree that I will press my case further with the international head of Taj Hotels once back in the UK. By now, we are in serious danger of missing the Lufthansa flight and the team is still not back from the court house. I phone them and tell them to come back immediately. Frank says he doesn't want to leave without all the tapes; I say they must. It is a very tough moment. I realise it is time for action, not ideals. I remind them that all along I have told them to trust me one hundred per cent – they have to do this now. I also ask Hassan to look after them and make their leaving as easy as possible.

Fortunately, they do return and we say a hasty goodbye to Sheikh Tariq in the hotel lobby. I compliment him and say he must be one of the cleverest men in Yemen. We rush off to the airport. Surely nothing can stop us now, though we have no time to waste before the plane takes off.

At the airport, there is hassle getting the camera gear through customs. All the paperwork has mysteriously disappeared but Hassan and James help smooth the way. Passport control is our final hurdle. Hassan and James watch us go to the counter and then make moves to leave. We go through the checkpoints OK, but the authorities refuse to give us our passports back. The plane is waiting on the tarmac and we are stuck.

"Hassan," I bellow. "Help!" He and James blag their way air-side to help negotiate. After a few minutes, I am summoned by an airport security chief. I am so determined to leave that I will do anything. He asks me whether I want to catch the flight – talk about a silly question!

"We *must* catch this flight," I growl.

"Well," he says, "we have a problem with Rageh Omaar."

"What problem?" I ask. He can't say. Both James and Hassan join me, and after lots of threats from Hassan in Arabic the official caves in.

I don't tell the guys what has happened until we take off. I don't want to load all the anxiety onto Rageh. All along we have stuck to our iron rule that we remain a united, cohesive group and I am not going to change that now. Once aboard, we slump into our seats and have a quiet drink, but we don't really relax until we hit the Red Sea and leave Yemeni airspace. Even then, I don't sleep a wink until we arrive at Heathrow eleven hours later.

CHAPTER SEVEN

Uncle Sam's Stalwarts

Over the last 25 years I have travelled to the Land of the Free on eight occasions, the majority of times for work. During this time, there is little doubt about what has been the biggest game-changing event in the United States – the 9/11 attacks by Al-Qaeda. These audacious and brutal assaults of course totally transformed the way America looked at itself and at the rest of the world. They also spawned a series of US military interventions in various parts of the globe, changing the lives of millions of people. I remember visiting the Twin Towers on my first visit to New York in 1987, and being overwhelmed by the scale and ambition of the buildings. It brought the shocking events of 9/11 even closer when I watched disbelievingly in my office at the BBC while the towers collapsed.

My only visit to the US since the atrocities came in 2008 when I took my 18-year-old daughter Bridget to New York so she could experience the thrilling bustle of American life for the first time. We visited the Ground Zero site, where preliminary work to build a new World Trade Centre and memorial was in full swing. Like thousands of others, we were moved to tears while wandering round the small memorial museum next to the scene of the Al Qaeda attacks.

Although I was not an eye witness to the 9/11 incidents, I did manage to see at close hand one of the other shifts in American history during modern times, as the Second World War generation of leaders moved off the political stage. I was in Washington in November 1988 when Margaret Thatcher went to say her formal goodbyes to President Reagan, who was about to hand over the reins of power to George Bush senior. Along with my reporter, the legendary Nick Clarke, I was able to watch a spectacular ceremony on the lawn at the back of the White House. It was my first and only visit to this bastion of Western democracy, and the occasion did not disappoint.

Given that Reagan and Thatcher were ideological soul-mates, who believed that they were winning the Cold War together, there was to be no stinting. The spacious lawn was packed full of marching military bands and there was an honour guard of soldiers for inspection, plus a 21-gun salute. I managed to take a few photographs of Nick right in the thick of the action. It was certainly stirring stuff, a political grand opera on a lavish scale, and seemed to celebrate what had been an historic turning point for the West in containing the threat of the Soviet empire.

As hundreds of invited well-wishers and journalists crowded around, the two leaders made short stirring speeches from a raised lectern placed on the grass. Both were in mutual congratulatory mood, though – true to form – Reagan's style was folksy and witty. He began thus:

"It's said that a cowboy went out riding one day and stumbled into the Grand Canyon, and he's supposed to have said, 'Wow, something sure has happened here.' (laughter) Well, Prime Minister Thatcher, when we contemplate the world as it is today and how it was when we first met eight years ago, we too have a right to say, 'something sure has happened.'"

In reply, Mrs Thatcher invoked the thoughts of one of America's founding fathers:

"Two hundred years ago, Tom Paine told the founders of this great nation, 'We have it in our power to begin the world over again.' Mr President, the office which you hold is the greatest in the world. But it is the man who holds the office – you, sir – who has enabled us to begin the world over again."

Of course, the two leaders had their critics, who said they were both overplaying their role on the world stage.

On the White House lawn with Margaret Thatcher being watched adoringly by President Reagan

But it was perhaps not since World War Two that an American President and British Prime Minister had formed such a close and effective partnership.

For our report for *Newsnight* on this love-in, we filmed some children from the Queen Anne School in Maryland, who performed a song for Mrs Thatcher. The music was greatly to her taste, as they sang, "*Accentuate the positive, eliminate the negative*".

It was my first opportunity to see Mrs Thatcher's infamous press spokesman in the flesh, the ebullient and plain-speaking Bernard Ingham. He gave one briefing for the press while standing on the pavement in central Washington, just inside a secure area portioned off from the general public.

We the press got as close as we could to the great man, but his voice was so low that I could hardly hear any of his words of wisdom.

Towards the end of this jamboree Nick Clarke did an interview with the woman of the moment, Mrs Thatcher. When he pressed her on how much the world had really changed during the Reagan/Thatcher years, she went on the offensive, pointing out a number of shifts, including progress in East-West arms control talks, the withdrawing of Soviet troops from Afghanistan and the growth in the world economy.

The American media did not devote that much attention to the sentimentality of this visit, but were more focused on what type of President George Bush would make when he took over from Reagan. Could he make the jump from a solid number two to being the main man? I was intrigued about this question too when I saw him dodging the limelight at the ceremony on the White House lawn. Of course, he turned out to be no wimp; he was to make his mark on the international stage with the successful leadership of the international coalition to drive the Iraqi leader Saddam Hussein out of Kuwait in 1991.

I was to see Bush again in the flesh at the Republican convention in Houston in 1992, shortly before he was defeated by Bill Clinton in the presidential elections a few months later. Viewing both Reagan and Bush in person meant I had witnessed the end of an era in American political life. The two men were followed by leaders who had not been alive during the Second World War and so had a completely new outlook on the world.

On other trips to Washington I also got the chance to meet some other towering figures from the Second World War generation; the spiky former Defence Secretary Caspar Weinberger, and the pugnacious and ambitious Secretary of State Al Haig. I even did an interview with Robert McNamara, the controversial Defence Secretary during the Vietnam War and former President of the World Bank. I spoke to him in the mid-eighties when producing that *Newsnight* item about the challenge posed to the West by the reforming Soviet leader, Mikhail Gorbachev. I remember being spellbound by this wizened and extremely clever elderly man sitting in his office next to a giant globe, as if it were passing comment on his territorial ambitions. Love them or hate them, all of these guys truly were some of Uncle Sam's greatest stalwarts.

I was sent to Houston for the Republican convention by *Newsnight*. It was held in the Astrodome, home of the Houston Astros baseball team. The preparations to turn the stadium into a party convention venue led to extensive disruption. *The Houston Chronicle* breathlessly reported that 29,000 of the seats had to be hidden by massive blue draping that formed the backdrop to the convention podium. Apparently, the stitching across the top and bottom of the fire-retardant, wrinkle-resistant curtain measured 11 miles. Because of the disruption caused by these elaborate preparations, the Astros were forced to play 26 consecutive away matches.

During the convention it was clear that Bush was fighting for his political life, as the fresh-faced Clinton was already proving to be a tough opponent. The showbiz hullabaloo surrounding the event was all on a much more energetic and grander scale than any of the party conferences I had been to in the UK.

The convention was also given added spice for the *Newsnight* team because it was attended by the incoming controversial BBC Director-General, John Birt. His presence was a significant distraction for the *Newsnight* presenter Jeremy Paxman and me, as we were wary of him closely inspecting our work, though we in turn were intrigued by the opportunity to study him at close quarters.

Looking back now more than twenty years on, it is this exposure to John Birt which dominates my memory of the Republican convention. In his own way, he too was a substantial agent of change and so it was intriguing to see him at close quarters in the crucible of the American political fray. What follows is my account of his visit that I wrote up shortly afterwards.

* * *

Birt, whose first wife was American, turns up for a couple of days while on holiday. Again, I am in the firing line, as I have forsaken my deputy editor's desk to direct *Newsnight*'s coverage on the ground. Birt immediately makes a beeline for Jeremy Paxman and engages him in conversation. These two have had their differences, as Birt hates what he regards as Jeremy's cheeky, arrogant line of questioning when tackling major political figures. However, Birt knows Paxman is a star and so finds it more congenial and potentially advantageous to talk to him rather than to me and the other two producers I am with.

I have already come across Birt a few times. The first occasion was when he toured the *Newsnight* office some time after he was appointed Deputy Director-General in 1987 to clean up the BBC's journalism. I was outputting the programme on the day that the former President of Pakistan, General Zia-ul-Haq, was assassinated when his plane was blown up. Birt was taller than I had imagined and was very off-putting in his body language. However, now in Houston, I am sure that he will not remember me. He is most certainly not a 'people person'.

However, we producers are very conscious of his judgemental presence and are somewhat abashed when he says he wants to watch us recording our segment for *Newsnight* on the next-to-last night of the convention. It just has to be our weakest contribution, of course; we have exhausted the underlying theme of the convention lurching to the right because it was felt that that was the only chance of getting Bush re-elected. Because of the time difference with London, we will also just miss the start of Bush's final rallying speech to the faithful. Nonetheless, the live insert goes reasonably well, despite our fears, and all would have been well if Birt had left then.

However, he chooses to stay on because he discovers that we have lined up a rare interview with Bush's high profile spokeswoman, Mary Matalin. She is a youngish, attractive, feisty lady, who has also gained some notoriety because she is romantically involved with the chief strategist of the rival Clinton campaign, James Carville. Because her interview has to be recorded before Bush's speech but will be transmitted after it, I want to keep her comments as short and general as possible, looking forward to the next stages of the campaign.

It is the type of interview we normally do on the hoof with a single camera, out of a studio environment. However, for practical reasons, Matalin wants to come to our little studio overlooking the convention floor. Birt is fully alert by now and we sense that he thinks this will be a full formal interview, when in fact I know I will only use a couple of clips lasting two minutes or so. We are looking for an answer about what tactics the Republican Party will adopt for the rest of the campaign, and also for some personal colour about how she can love a man who, in political terms, is a sworn enemy.

However, Birt has already taken it upon himself to begin to brief Paxman on how to map out a line of attack – an approach he made famous in the *Weekend World* analytical programme, which was highly structured and complex.

"You should ask her why the convention hasn't allowed more debate from the floor," he suggests. It is a valid enough question, though I know it would be backward-looking by the time the interview is aired the following night in the UK.

Worse is to come. Birt seems to be working himself into full battle status, as if reliving his glory days when he produced David Frost's interview with the disgraced American President Richard Nixon.

"And when she denies that, you should go on to say..." he continues. At this point, Birt stops himself and realises that maybe he is getting too involved. "No, I'd better leave you to it."

Paxman, who is well aware of the jokes about the Birtist method of preparing interviews with precise algebraic formulae covering a legion of possible lines of questioning, perhaps should play a straight bat. Instead, to his own horror, he cannot help himself and finds that his impish sense of humour gets the better of him.

"That sounds too Birtist to me," he quips. I do not dare look at Birt's face to see his reaction.

During the interview, I can sense that the watching Birt expects me to have worked out a detailed script of questions with Paxman and be constantly on the talk-back into Paxman's ear, hollering the next googly of a question. My approach on this occasion is to intervene little, unless there is a major reason for doing so. After all, I have told Jeremy what I want and, in any case, Matalin has said she can stay for only a few minutes.

Soon Jeremy gets her to comment on one of our two key points: her news-making relationship with James Carville. He makes a clever reference to a contemporary film, *Sleeping with the Enemy*, starring Julia Roberts, and rather wittily asks Matalin how she copes with sleeping with her own Republican enemy. It is an entertaining and illuminating question and justifiably gossipy, but certainly not a very Birtist one. Out of the corner of my eye, I can see the new DG grimacing. It does not faze Matalin though, and she is happy to stay much longer than planned, by which time the interview has indeed become a bit unstructured and unfocused.

As we leave our mini studio, I hold my head in my hands. I know that Birt has been critical in the past about *Newsnight* because he believed the presenters were not briefed properly when doing major set-piece interviews. In some cases he was right, and here I am, the programme's deputy editor, apparently revealing to him that not enough thought has gone into doing an interview. On top of that, he has already been openly teased by Paxman. As we leave the studio and head back to our little office, Jeremy and I commiserate each other, but we end up having a good laugh about the whole incident.

Suddenly Jeremy freezes. I turn in despair to see the shuffling though silent gait of Birt, who has caught up with us, presumably to give his own post mortem about the interview. He must have heard us making fun of the incident, but mercifully says nothing about it.

Later on during Bush's speech to the convention, I have another first hand dose of Birtism in action. Bush is rambling and failing to ignite the party faithful. Birt watches the speech in the BBC studio, which is transmitting live on the BBC's international television channel. Suddenly, Birt, the arch proponent of structured and analytical thought, can contain himself no longer. In front of our team he utters his immortal verdict on the Bush performance.

"This speech is hopeless. What has happened to his structure?" he says, while we all try very hard to keep a straight face.

CHAPTER EIGHT

Political Earthquakes at Home

For the last twenty years I have focused mainly on international news during my professional career, and so I have witnessed very recent British history as a mere punter, rather than as a journalist. That means that I have had no inside track on key events such as the campaign against Blair's war in Iraq, and the impact of the financial crash of 2008 on the British economy.

However, in the early part of my career at the BBC during the eighties and early nineties, I concentrated mainly on domestic issues, so I had a front row seat to many of the political and social changes in the UK during this time. My first assignment out of the *Newsnight* office was to set up a discussion during the miners' strikes of 1984-85, an event which had a profound effect on British workers and communities. My task was to assemble a discussion in Sheffield involving striking miners and some pitmen from the coalfields of Nottinghamshire, who were staying at work in protest over the lack of a strike ballot. Not surprisingly, there was much venom between the participants. There was nearly an ugly riot when striking miners were collecting their BBC expenses and discovered that their "scab" counterparts would also be receiving them. It was a salutary introduction to life on location away from the safe if frenetic confines of the *Newsnight* office and studio.

In the eighties, I met a succession of Tory cabinet ministers, such as Ken Clarke, Michael Heseltine, Norman Tebbit and Douglas Hurd, who periodically traipsed into the *Newsnight* studios to defend the Conservative government. Like many other producers on the show, I was also on the receiving end of several bullying phone calls from the Labour publicity supremo, Peter Mandelson. When I was deputy editor of *Newsnight*, I also had a phone call from Gordon Brown, who at the time was a rising star in the opposition. He was complaining about coverage of the Labour Party and was rude and unpleasant throughout our conversation. He even threatened to report me to the Director-General for my unsympathetic response to his demands – so I was not surprised that, years later when he was in office as prime minister, stories began to circulate of alleged volcanic temper tantrums in front of his staff.

Margaret Thatcher dominated this period with her attacks on the power of trade unions and her attempts to create a share-owning public. We are still feeling the aftershocks of the Big Bang liberalisation of the City in 1987 today. When Mrs Thatcher was forced out of office in 1990, *Newsnight* went into overdrive with its analysis of the changing face of British politics.

In this chapter, I will focus on three episodes which highlighted the continuing reverberations following her dramatic exit – the election of John Major as her successor, Britain's ungainly and chaotic departure from the European Exchange Rate Mechanism in 1992, and the election of Tony Blair in 1997. I witnessed all of these events at close quarters.

THE RISE OF JOHN MAJOR – A SNAPSHOT

The unexpected and swift departure of Mrs Thatcher from the political landscape was a truly pivotal transition in the fortunes of the UK and the Conservative Party. The atmosphere in the *Newsnight* office in the aftermath of her resignation was feverish and memorable. I leapt at the chance to go with my old mucker Peter Snow to interview one of the fast-emerging favourites to take over from her – John Major, the then Chancellor of the Exchequer. He had been recovering at his home near Huntingdon after reportedly having his wisdom teeth removed. Some said this was merely an excuse to take him away from the London political hothouse of plotting and counter-plotting, but we nevertheless went to 11 Downing Street and were ushered in to see the man of the moment, who had sneaked back into town.

The interview had been arranged at short notice and, although Peter and I were respectably dressed, the crew turned up in their usual scruffy garb of jeans and casual shirts. I was a bit embarrassed on their behalf and was intrigued to see how Major would handle it. When I once had produced an interview with Peter Snow with Margaret Thatcher in her prime ministerial pomp, she had ignored every member of the crew. Peter's attempt to engage her in some casual chit-chat before the formal interview was given the brush off. She sat in silence composing herself and refusing to utter anything that could be seized on as an indiscretion.

To my great astonishment, Major was completely different. He introduced himself in turn to all the team, shaking our hands in welcome and looking each one of us in the eye. Even our cynical and world-weary lighting man was visibly impressed by this show of warm humility.

An even bigger surprise was to follow. As Major and Snow sat opposite each other waiting for the cameraman to set up his equipment, the pretender to the throne leaned over to Peter and asked him where the make-up lady was. He wanted to guard against any undue sweating and look good on camera. Major had mistakenly thought this encounter was going to be a full outside broadcast, complete with a big crew. Instead, we were just a small mobile unit and so had no make-up facilities. Fortunately, Snow came to the rescue and discovered in his pocket a small make-up compact powder box, which he offered to Major.

I had to pinch myself as Major, presumably still in pain after his wisdom teeth operation, gingerly started to pat his cheeks and murmured aloud: "Gently does it, gently does it... Oh, this could be a good political credo." After the no-nonsense and shrill prime ministerial style of Mrs Thatcher, it was staggering to see someone eulogising about what seemed to be such a limp and starkly contrasting vision.

However, I was left in no doubt that we were definitely going to enter a new era if Major won the subsequent leadership election, which he duly did. I thought about this mantra many times when he was later lampooned in office for being such a grey personality and was characterised as a man who tucked his shirt into his underpants. His gentle, mild-mannered approach somehow got him elected against the odds in the 1992 general election. I had a ringside seat at this victory, as I was in editorial charge of all 96 BBC outside broadcasts on the night. This entailed having a thrilling rollercoaster ride at the top of a huge pyramid of communication networks from the various counts and key locations across Britain.

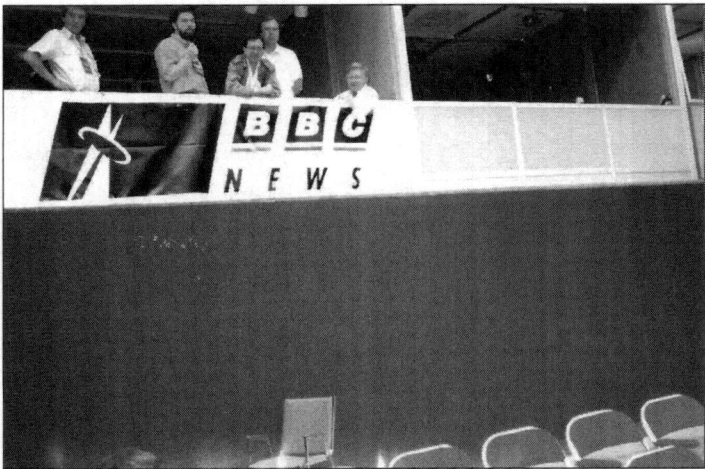

Pausing with BBC colleagues during a rehearsal for the 1992 General Election programme. The presenter David Dimbleby is on the extreme right.

It should have been a significant turning point in the British political scene with a Labour win, but the Tories' unexpected victory was probably more due to Kinnock's personal unpopularity than a triumph for Major's low-key approach. But "gently does it" did not help him throughout his tempestuous rule in trying to subdue the rebellious voices in his party, including some unnamed cabinet members he once unguardedly referred to as bastards.

EUROPEAN MONEY TROUBLES

One of Major's biggest problems was trying to keep his party united on the tricky issue of Europe. At this stage, most of the rest of the European community was hell bent on creating closer economic and political ties. Many of Major's party were vehemently against such integration and were not afraid to say so loudly.

The bi-annual European summits took on extra significance in this period, and *Newsnight* was represented in force at each of them. I went to Rome in December 1990, the first summit for John Major as prime minister. It was all rather downbeat. Margaret Thatcher had exploded at the previous summit and her intransigence had contributed to her downfall. In Rome, Major tried to bind the wounds she had caused and was in no mood to rock the boat, so it was a dull affair. The only bit of excitement for me came after I had to grab the then Dutch Prime Minister, Ruud Lubbers, for an interview. I took him to a quiet room to meet the waiting crew, only to find the cameraman had fallen asleep. Red faces all around.

Although the Rome summit went reasonably well for John Major, by the autumn of 1992 he had been badly wounded by his European policies, as many Tory prime ministers had been before him. According to his lights,

Major had had a triumph at the Maastricht summit earlier in the year, when he had negotiated two treaty opt-outs for Britain on the social chapter and common currency, a move still causing ripples around the European Union and Westminster to this day. However, the subsequent guerrilla warfare with some of his recalcitrant backbenchers had left him severely mauled.

Major's European reputation also became battered by Britain's forced exit from the European Exchange Rate Mechanism in September 1992, on what came to be known as Black Wednesday. The ERM was aimed at reducing variations in exchange rates and was a forerunner of the European single currency. Britain had joined the mechanism in 1990, but had to leave just two years later in an embarrassing departure. However, looking back now with the benefit of hindsight, some political analysts believe that the UK's exit from the ERM was a blessing in disguise, as it brought economic freedoms and benefits. At the time, though, it was an unmitigated political disaster for the Major government.

Black Wednesday on 16 September 1992 was one of those frenetic amazing days at *Newsnight* when you really felt at the centre of events. The editor, Tim Gardam, was away on holiday in France and the other deputy editor, Eamonn Matthews, had left the programme, so I was in total charge. As the day dawned, I had a feeling a big story was in the air. I was determined to get totally involved in the day's editorial decisions, instead of taking a more strategic view and leaving a lot of the nitty-gritty to the editor of the day.

It was a rollercoaster day, with the pound coming under sustained pressure from currency speculators. But no-one foresaw that the panic-stricken government would first push up interest rates from ten to twelve per cent and then to 15 per cent, in a bid to stave off predatory speculators. As each desperate move was announced, I would frequently rush out of my little glass box office into the main office and exchange incredulous glances with the editor of the day, Jim Gray.

One of the interviewees we had already signed up by early afternoon was the former Labour Prime Minister Lord Callaghan, who had experienced similar buffetings when he was Chancellor of the Exchequer in 1967. The arrangements for the interview were complicated, especially as he wanted to pre-record it from his home in East Sussex. This posed a considerable challenge, as this was before the days when satellite links were cheap and easily available in the UK.

Instead, we sent a crew and a producer down to East Sussex, got Jeremy Paxman to pose the interview questions from London and then send the recorded material of Callaghan's answers back from a feed point on the South Downs. On an already hectic day, this operation put severe strain on our limited resources. The crew was late in reaching Lord Callaghan and so he was already in a tetchy mood when the interview was recorded at around 5pm. Meanwhile, we were under increasing pressure to set up the rest of the programme and – not surprisingly – we were finding it difficult to line up a Conservative government spokesman, as all the ministers were trying to keep their heads down.

By around 7.45pm all our plans had to be thrown into the air when the Chancellor Norman Lamont sheepishly announced that Britain was suspending its membership of the ERM. I had another exchange of amazed glances with Jim Gray. The running order had to be completely rewritten and we agonised over what to do about Lord Callaghan. His interview had clearly been taken over by events and we could not run it in its present form. It would make him and us look very silly and out of touch. So would he be prepared to do another interview? Could we put the machinery back in place to transmit back from the South Downs?

In the end, Jim rang Lord Callaghan to explain what had happened and he agreed to do a live interview on the phone when the programme was transmitted late in the evening. As Jim and I tore our hair out trying to wrestle the programme into some sort of shape, we fell back on that producer's crucial maxim when confronted with a breaking story that is spiralling out of control: get some bums on seats in the studio as live guests. Forget trying to do too many fancy pre-recorded pieces, as they would have to be thrown away. I was well aware of the embarrassment that would be caused if we messed up this edition of *Newsnight* on such a momentous, game-changing day. I was in sole charge, so the pressure was truly on.

On big nights like this, *Newsnight* always had a much larger audience and the serried ranks of senior BBC bosses would also be unusually attentive. To give us cover, I grabbed the BBC Economics Editor Peter Jay when he finished his piece on the *Nine O'Clock News*. Peter, who ironically used to be Lord Callaghan's son-in-law, readily agreed to be a live studio guest. Despite Jay's alleged aloof persona and closeness to Birtist philosophy, I came to respect his expertise and benefited from the sophisticated and authoritative economic briefings he gave to the daily gathering of senior BBC editors. He was, though, something of an enigma. A year before the ERM crisis, I came across him standing one dark evening outside in the central circle at Television Centre, shortly after the body of his former boss, the newspaper magnate Robert Maxwell, had been found floating in the Atlantic Ocean. Jay looked completely forlorn and wistful, smoking a cigarette. He had been Maxwell's Chief of Staff and obviously the death of a close professional colleague was bound to be destabilising.

On the night of the ERM debacle, we also jacked up a live interview spot from the BBC reporter Jonathan Charles, who was covering a late-night meeting of European finance officials in Brussels. Now all we needed was to set up a UK government spokesman for a live interview. At first, it seemed as if no-one would be prepared to appear on any outlet in the BBC. Then the party chairman Norman Fowler was offered up as a sacrificial lamb to news programmes. Annoyingly, he refused to come on to *Newsnight*, probably fearing that he would come off a poor second to Jeremy Paxman, who was champing at the bit over such a tumultuous story.

After much huffing and puffing, Conservative Central Office put up another scapegoat, Tim Smith, one of the vice-chairmen of the party. It was a big mistake; he was roasted by Paxman, as he spluttered and mumbled his way through an attempt to defend a Tory Prime Minister who could one week say that leaving the ERM would be fool's gold and the next week flee the mechanism in disgrace. We kept Tim Smith in the studio throughout the programme, and Paxman periodically returned to inflict more humiliation on him. As the Observer television critic John Naughton memorably wrote in his column afterwards, Paxman had been magnificent in "cuffing" the hapless Tim Smith.

The programme overall went reasonably well. However, because so much was still unfolding as we were live on air, it was forty minutes into the show before we managed to take the live phone interview with Lord Callaghan. Then, for timing and technical reasons, the interview had to be cut short. As we came off air, I shared in the euphoria of the production team in delivering what we thought to have been gripping television on such a dramatic day. But I already had a niggling feeling that something would have to be done about Lord Callaghan. After any fast-moving show, several egos usually have to be massaged as guests get dropped, pre-recorded pieces are butchered and the ground rules of discussions change. The relentless momentum of a huge story could leave individuals feeling bruised and abused, and I often had to make apologies to presenters, production staff and/or interviewees. Because of the possible repercussions of having a testy Lord Callaghan on the war path, I realised I had better make a quick attempt to smooth any ruffled feathers. Senior politicians invariably have massive egos, and as for former prime ministers ...!

On this occasion, any indignities suffered had been nobody's fault, as the historic calamitous events of the day had inevitably led to many rethinks. Nevertheless, I made myself wake up early the next morning to compose a courteous, grovelling letter to Lord Callaghan. I tried to be as polite and respectful as possible, though concluded the letter by pointing out that in many ways we had simply been at the mercy of events. I then shoved this little local difficulty to the back of my mind, feeling that I had done my duty and that would be the end of it.

In the meantime, I had to throw myself into *Newsnight*'s coverage of the day after the night before. By this stage, my brain was in overdrive as we agonised about how to come up with an intelligent theme for that night's programme. In the end, we constructed the show around two central questions: had the government now got an economic policy, and had the government now got a European policy? This programme was also successful, as were other follow-up shows for the rest of the week, so I went into work each day feeling pretty pleased with life. But my state of well-being did not last long.

On my desk soon arrived a letter written on House of Lords notepaper. It was from an irate Lord Callaghan; he was furious with me about what he said had been the discourtesy shown to him – the initial late arrival of the crew at his farm, the scrapping of the first interview, the lateness of the hour of his eventual live phone interview and the miserly time given to it. In conclusion, he lectured me on the value of politeness, manners and keeping one's word. He said it was easy to keep high standards when all was well: the test of good faith was that one stuck with agreements even when the going got tough. *On that account, you have failed,* he wrote. Just the sort of letter you need at the start of the day. He was anything but 'Sunny Jim', one of his pet nicknames used by the press.

I also noticed that his letter was copied to the Director-General, John Birt, in an apparent attempt to intimidate me and get me into trouble. In my early BBC career, I would have been mortified and panic-stricken, but by now I was battle-hardened and did not feel cowed by such bullying. I could understand how frustrated Lord Callaghan must have been by the changes and delays, which is why I had apologised for them. However, I was disappointed that a man who had carried the affairs of the nation on his shoulders should apparently resort to such pettiness and seemed unwilling to acknowledge that the power of historical forces was far bigger than any one individual. To be fair to Birt, he did not cause any trouble over this complaint. He passed the letter to the head of news and current affairs, Tony Hall, and simply scrawled on the bottom of the letter *Another satisfied customer.* When Hall's office contacted me and I explained the whole story, I heard nothing more of it.

Soon I forgot the whole Callaghan episode. The fall-out of the withdrawal from the ERM put John Major's leadership under severe strain and the programme was desperately busy reporting on the fissures that were opening up in the Tory party. The manoeuvrings over the paving motion for the debate on the Maastricht treaty kept us going for days. When it came to the crucial vote in the Commons, I again left my little glass box office at *Newsnight* to go down to Westminster to edit our live inject from the Millbank studio. It was all very tense as we waited for the vote, and again we operated our defensive bums-on-seats policy by having two Lords, Prior and Tebbit, in the studio reacting to events. Lord Prior was a former Tory cabinet minister and was seen as one of the 'wets', who disagreed with many of the tenets of Thatcherism. However, Lord Tebbit, as one of Mrs Thatcher's most enthusiastic supporters, hated the Maastricht treaty.

In the end, the government had a majority of just three. During the programme a troupe of MPs arrived to take part in the show after streaming out of the lobbies. One of them was another former prime minister, Ted Heath, and there was a delicate moment when he spotted his Thatcherite arch-enemy, Tebbit, dubbed the 'Chingford skinhead'. He hissed with venom in his direction. Fortunately, Tebbit had already left the studio set as his contribution was over. It was a good job. Whether Heath would have sat for long in the same studio as the Chingford skinhead was very dubious, so it was a narrow escape.

I relished all this hands-on experience, as I was coming to the end of my time on *Newsnight*. My last assignment was to oversee the European summit a few weeks later in Edinburgh. It gave me the chance to be on the road again with Peter Snow; he was in fine form, recording live links from outside Hollyrood House and running around corridors trying to inveigle government ministers and officials into releasing juicy titbits about the progress of the talks. However, he did not reach the dizzy heights of his performance at the Maastricht summit itself six months previously when – so legend has it – he had cornered the Chancellor Norman Lamont in the gents and asked for a quote.

On the final night of the summit in Scotland, Lamont agreed to give us a more official interview, this time in the plush surroundings of his hotel lobby. However, there was a hiccup; Lamont was running late, as he was attending a formal dinner hosted by the Queen aboard the royal yacht, Britannia. Princess Diana was also in attendance, just days after John Major had announced her official separation from Prince Charles. Once again, Snow was in his element. He spied the European minister, Tristan Garel-Jones, who had returned to the hotel early and persuaded him to talk to us on camera. It was just as well, because Lamont then officially cried off from doing a live interview. To preserve our honour, we still lurked near the hotel entrance to try to snatch a doorstep interview with him when he returned.

Somehow we managed to be the only journalists in the hotel, which by now was filling up with an array of Euro dignitaries. One of them was the President of the Commission, Jacques Delors, whose bodyguard brusquely shoved me out of the way as his boss approached. Delors marched past with an air of Gallic superiority and withering disdain for me, a creature of the low-life media, who had had the effrontery of getting in his way. The message of the earlier infamous *Sun* headline, '*Up Yours Delors*' never seemed more appropriate.

We continued to hover in the hotel lobby to pounce on Lamont, and our patience was rewarded with Snow extracting a brief news clip from him about inflation. By now, other leading politicians were also mingling in the lobby, still bedecked in their evening dress finery after the Britannia bash. The irrepressible Snow also accosted the Foreign Secretary Douglas Hurd who betrayed his Eton breeding as he stood with a ramrod straight back when facing the camera. We were also treated to a glimpse of John Major himself, his 'gently does it' mantra now under severe strain. However, he did seem much more self-assured than when we had seen him in Downing Street.

Suddenly it was all over. The broadcast coverage passed without any incident and that was virtually the end of my *Newsnight* career. I did manage to sign off with a memorable final interviewee scalp, as I had to do a quick pre-recorded session with the former President of France, Valéry Giscard d'Estaing, while Peter was preoccupied with something else. In a skilful and elegant way, he urged Major to stop all the foot-dragging over the Maastricht Treaty and said the delays had not produced a positive image for Britain. He also encouraged his successor, President Mitterrand, and other leaders to put pressure on the UK to help complete the European project as soon as possible. Given the continuing alarms and excursions between Britain and the European Union right up to the time this book was written, it seems that his words were as effective as the proverbial pissing in the wind.

Overall, I was too shattered at the end of the summit to be too wistful. We did manage to have a bottle of champagne at a bustling Italian restaurant out on the town. I did not get the chance to savour this moment too much, as we were interrupted by a group of drunken Scotsmen demanding Snow's autograph. At the hotel a few of us drank whisky way into the night before collapsing into bed. It seemed a very limp way to go out after nine years on *Newsnight* during which I had had the chance to see many influential agents of change at close quarters.

However, there was to be one final sting in the tail. On entering the plane back to London the next day, I was astonished to lock eyes with a young lady dressed in a demure black suit, sitting on the first seat at the front of the aircraft. The shy, sensitive soul in front of me was none other than the Princess of Wales, sloping off back to London after attending that dinner on the Britannia. Presumably, after her separation from Prince Charles, travelling on public transport was now to be her fate from time to time. Much had happened to her since I had last seen her at the film festival in Cannes in 1987. Our stations in life were vastly different of course, but like me, she had come to the end of an era.

BLAIR COMES TO POWER

One of my final assignments on location in the UK came on election day in May 1997. I was delighted to be offered the task of producing the outside broadcast coverage at the Royal Festival Hall on the banks of the Thames, where Labour planned to hold an event which they hoped would turn into a victory party. It was a fun assignment, but not a particularly easy one.

The first challenge came when the main programme was not able to take live a performance of the Labour party song, *Things Can Only Get Better*, performed at the party by D:REAM, with the now famous physicist Brian Cox as one of the band members. I was asked to see whether the group would perform the song again, just for television. I took a deep breath and began negotiations. The band agreed, but I was then told by Television Centre that they did not have time to take it after all. When being part of a huge live programme, it is always good to remember the words of Gloucester in Macbeth: "As flies to wanton boys are we to the gods. They kill us for their sport."

The next challenge was fighting with the formidable Christiane Amanpour of CNN to carry out an interview with a senior Labour figure, Robin Cook. As he walked up some stairs, she had hold of one of his arms and I grabbed the other one. We were delighted when Cook agreed to talk to the BBC first.

It was quickly becoming clear that Labour was on course for a handsome victory and so the excitement built at the party. It was definitely the place to be. As dawn was breaking on a beautiful spring day, the Labour faithful gathered outside on the terrace to wait for the arrival of Tony Blair, the newly elected prime minister. I was also among the crowd and felt overwhelmed by the ecstatic cheering when Blair hove into view. It was great to be right at the centre of the action, to see a transfer of power with my own eyes.

Later, I was asked to go produce the coverage from an outside broadcast unit outside Blair's private house in Islington. It meant I had no sleep, but who cared on a night such as this? While waiting for Blair to come out of his house to go to the Palace, I went into a nearby newspaper shop to buy some snacks for breakfast to keep me going. The shop owner was telling all and sundry that he knew the Blair family well and the new PM's kids came in regularly to buy penny sweets. I thought that perhaps Blair might not be that bad as prime minister if he had some awareness of the realities and demands of normal family life. Back at the house, the waiting crowd saw an embarrassed and bleary-eyed Cherie Blair being photographed in her nightie as she opened the door to accept a delivery of flowers.

Among the many well-wishers gathering on the street in the early morning sun, there was much optimism and hope. Looking back now, it is hard to equate this mood with the current attitudes towards Blair, who many feel let his country down by going to war with Saddam Hussein on trumped-up evidence about the presence of weapons of mass destruction. When Blair finally emerged from his house to go to see the Queen, there was a huge roar of acclamation. Despite my fatigue, it certainly felt like the dawning of a new era.

CHAPTER NINE

The Price of Gold

I never expected to be able to undertake an expedition to the Amazon rainforest in Brazil. My work at the BBC mainly dealt with international politics and current affairs, and a journey to such exotic climes did not seem on the radar. However, when I temporarily escaped BBC management duties after leaving *Newsnight* at the end of 1992, I had the chance to make a documentary for the *BBC Assignment* programme about the changing face of the Amazon. What had caught my eye were the reports of the rampant destruction of the rainforest because of illegal logging and gold mining. This, after all, was current affairs in its widest sense. Here was a massive unfolding environmental story about one of the greatest natural wonders of the world. Filming in the region would also guarantee a strong adventure story which hopefully would make a gripping documentary.

I was thrilled when the idea was accepted, and I decided to focus on the activities of the garimpeiros, or illegal gold diggers. One important issue was how the unrestrained use of mercury to separate out gold particles from river mud was damaging the river systems and even threatening human health, as many fish were now being contaminated by the mercury. I could not wait to get going as I read blood curdling tales of how up to a million garimpeiros were caught up in gold fever and were threatened by malaria, pestilence and violence.

I spent five weeks in all in the Amazon. In the first two weeks I carried out a research trip aided by the ever-cheerful Guardian correspondent in Brazil, Jan Rocha. We were later joined by the camera crew and the authoritative reporter, Julian Pettifer, who had become famous while covering the Vietnam War, but in later years had developed an expertise in covering environmental issues. The 45-minute documentary we made was called *The Price of Gold,* and was shown on BBC2 and BBC World.

I kept a diary of my various adventures in the Amazon in 1993 while travelling extensively across the region from the mouth of the river to the deepest interior. Some places were visited twice – once for a recce and once for filming. An abridged version of the diary follows below. It is not organised in a strict chronology, but is grouped around some key places that we travelled to.

ARRIVAL AT RIO AIRPORT – TUESDAY 24 AUGUST 1993

Because we are going to places where only cash rules, I have to bring enough money for our transport and to pay the local crew. In all, I have 27,000 US dollars on me, including travellers cheques, but am carrying more than half the full amount in cash. I feel like some Mafia hoodlum on a special mission. This amount of cash obviously calls for an elaborate security plan. A bundle of US greenbacks goes into a pouch worn round my neck. I stuff some more notes into a tubular bandage on my left leg – a very crafty dodge advocated by some tropical travel writers. Some is jammed into my shirt top pocket, some in the orthodox position in my wallet, with the rest safely hidden in a new shoulder wallet, which fits neatly against the body, as if I am carrying a gun in a holster like a gangster, Nevertheless, I am glad to be met by a local researcher with a car, as I am worried about thieves at the airport.

The traffic is much better than expected and we whizz through a tunnel system to the world-famous Copacabana beach, and the white-fronted Palace Hotel where Orson Welles apparently once threw a piano out of a window. The building reminds me of the Carlton Hotel on the Croisette in Cannes. The beach, though, is much more spectacular, dominated by massive Atlantic rollers. It is great to be kept in such style. But I don't feel too guilty; with our special BBC rate of 100 dollars a night, it is as cheap as staying in a functional business hotel in Mansfield. The swimming pool is very enticing, so I do a few lengths despite the cold water and go for a stroll along the beach. Life is hell sometimes!

BELÉM – WEDNESDAY 25 AUGUST

In the evening, we catch a flight from Rio to the Amazon. It takes four hours to fly to the town of Belém. As we arrive, I get a glimpse in the moonlight of one of the channels of the river; it is a thrilling, tantalising foretaste of what is to come. We stay at the Hilton Hotel, a huge monstrosity, devoid of character, but it is clean and air-conditioned. I am exhausted, so sleep comes easily.

The next day I have my first glimpse of the Amazon River in daylight, though strictly speaking it is not the Amazon proper here. Belém is on a tributary, but even so the river is still far wider than the Thames in London. The tributary leads to one of the main channels around an island in the mouth of the river. I wake at six and am surprised to see it is already light. The waterfront is bustling, as is the centre of the town – a fascinating mixture of English, Portuguese and Amazonian influences. The Brits have left lovely squares with gardens and the ironwork for the extensive market by the waterfront. The Portuguese have left the fort by the harbour and many elegant colonial buildings. The local influences provide a lot of character, but also rubbish-strewn, smelly streets on the outskirts.

In the morning we go to the market near the fort, which bustles with activity. It looks chaotic, though on careful inspection you can tell that informal hierarchies are operating. After a while I spot a kingpin orchestrating the various bidders for fish, fruit, vegetables and nuts. A host of young men with grimy faces scatter everywhere carrying boxes of produce on their heads – and woe betide you if you don't get out of their way. Gangs of pickpockets are also in evidence; one or two of them cause an obstruction and diversion, allowing another one to pounce. I manage to stop one inquiring hand from delving into my pocket in search of bank notes. Fortunately, I have left my huge stash of cash at the hotel.

Dozens of battered boats are moored alongside the market. Some have dirty hammocks, swaying in the breeze. On one boat there is the squealing of terrified pigs, trussed up by the legs awaiting the executioner's knife, a buyer and the cooking pot. A few of the pigs are lying pathetically on the quay, panic-stricken. No sympathy is doled out to them as several passers-by give them a kick, just for the hell of it. The temperature in the middle of the day is about 36 degrees and so we slope off for a siesta.

Later, we go to the airport to fly up river to Santarém. We take off for the jungle expecting the worst about various horrors that might lie ahead in the interior. But no, Santarém is all very civilised. We are met by a van which takes us to the Tropical Hotel, a huge rambling edifice that is a cross between a football stadium and a flying saucer. The hotel has wood floors and mercifully has air conditioning and big rooms. The large circular pool outside is spectacular. We have dinner with Dr Branches, who is concerned about the impact on health of the unfettered use of mercury, which can find its way into the food chain. Despite this, I happily eat the fish on the menu. The doctor has a good sense of humour and deep scepticism of scientists and local politicians, all wanting to make their names out of the mercury issue.

ITAITUBA – SATURDAY 28 AUGUST

An early start dawns in Santarém. After a fitful night's sleep, I am excited to wake around 5.30am and be able to glimpse the beautiful blue waters of the Tapajos, an Amazon tributary. We eat breakfast by the pool – the usual concoction of fresh fruit, rolls, eggs and ham, with cafe com leite. Delicious!

Today we are going into the interior and have to catch an air taxi to Itaituba. The plane seats about twenty people and is twin-engined, much to my relief. There are only three passengers, so we sit at the front and are treated like royalty by the captain. We follow the Tapajos all the way down. At first, it is very wide with a bright blue tinge. About two thirds of the way down, it becomes narrower and changes colour to a lightish blue-grey, courtesy of the garimpeiros. On either side of the river, trees stretch for miles. Much of the landscape looks like virgin forest, with only the odd dirt track and clearings for crops and animals. I am surprised by the number of small hills which pop up here and there, improving the landscape.

The pilot tells us hair-raising tales about other small planes in the area, many of which are badly-maintained. Single-engine planes especially are seen as death traps. After 45 minutes we arrive in Itaitubua, having been fortified by a cup of hot chocolate from a flask. The airport is compact, with a small control tower, and is surprisingly efficient and clean. The town, however, is very wild, with lots of bars and dodgy individuals loafing around in shop doorways. There are many poor areas, with hordes of barefoot children running around in the dirt and open sewers running down the streets. The Hotel Juliana is amazingly good, though. It has a very clean, tiled floor with air conditioning, a TV and a rudimentary fridge in the room – all this for around eleven dollars a night. We can't complain.

The hotel is right by the waterfront and I go for a stroll. There is a makeshift market and some higgledy-piggledy docking facilities where lumbering river boats tie up. The water edge is filthy, with floating litter and excrement, though it could be made into an appealing promenade area with a little money and care. A refreshing breeze blows but it is still very hot.

There has been rain here for the first time in ages and this has blown away a lot of low cloud and mist caused by forest fires. Jan and I try to hire a little launch with a petrol engine to go down river a few miles to a village called Brasilia Legal, where Dr Branches has found some high mercury levels in the population. We fail at our first attempt to negotiate a rate. The men want 120 US dollars, far more than the flight from Santarém, so a stalemate ensues and we will have to return. We have lunch at a local café where we tuck into huge portions of rice, fried bananas and peas.

We return to the waterfront and this time make a more acceptable deal with a boatman. His craft is a simple pirogue with an outboard motor; it is rather flimsy but we speed in a pleasing way through the grey-blue Tapajos waters. Brasilia Legal is 45 miles away – a half-hour ride. There are some life jackets but Jan and I are in a blasé mood, infected by the freedom and enticing sensation of the breeze in our faces as we gaze across the water and to the forest on the bank. We come to our senses when our guide hits a sandbank near an island a couple of miles downriver. We hastily put on our jackets, trying not to think about the consequences of tipping over into the water; crocodiles, pollution, maybe even piranhas. We drift for a few minutes but fortunately all is well and we speed on our way again.

The bench of the boat is very hard, so soon we have a classic numb bum feeling. From time to time, we see some river dolphins leaping lazily out of the water, their black fins standing out starkly in the sunlight. We also pass the occasional riverboat. They are like something out of a Mark Twain novel on the Mississippi, though their paintwork is dirty. There are several islands in the river before we come to Brasilia Legal. The first thing we see of the settlement is a house built in 1909, doubling as a post office. The village is strung along the bank, high out of reach of the flood water line. Most houses are pretty ramshackle. A number of boats are tethered on ropes to the shore and a couple of young boys are setting off in a tiny boat with fishing nets.

All in all, it is a very sleepy atmosphere. We find the head of the village trying to mend his boat but it is unlikely to be in action for a long time, as it needs major repairs. In the meantime, he prefers to take life easy and earn his living by doing odd jobs. You don't need much to survive here, apart from good health. He invites us into his house, which is very simple with chairs made of wire, and bare walls and floors. The only decoration is a china dog.

The leader knows about the mercury problem but feels helpless. The people have to eat fish and there is nothing they can do, he says. A group of children takes us on a guided tour to the school and telephone exchange. The phone is ringing but no-one answers it. There is also the occasional shop selling cans of milk and bottles of coke, and an array of household implements, including gleaming pots and menacing-looking machetes. We decide it will be a good place to film. The river is rougher on the way back;

every so often, the boat comes down on the water with a loud thud, jarring our spines. The sun is very hot and, despite my hat, suntan lotion, and insect repellent, I can feel myself getting burnt.

Once back, we go for a much-needed siesta in our rooms. I am woken up by cheering about an hour later. It turns out that the Brazilian football team is playing Bolivia in a World Cup qualifier and Brazil has just scored the first goal. Jan and I go to a nearby bar to watch the rest of the game. The place stinks but is friendly enough and, as Brazil score more goals, the cheers grow louder. It is six-nil in the end. Towards the end of the game, a group of about ten men arrives on the back of a lorry, waving a Brazilian flag. We shake their hands and they chant *Brasil, Brasil* incessantly. It is such a morale booster for the whole country when Brazil does well. As we walk the streets afterwards, everyone seems to have a spring in their step.

A couple of weeks later, we return to Itaituba with our crew and correspondent, Julian Pettifer. On the flight over, we go over Brasilia Legal itself, where we can see clearly the difference in the colour of the water between mining and non-mining areas. Once we land, we take two boats this time from Itaituba to Brasilia Legal. I go with the camera crew and we take our time filming the wake of the boat and some river scenes, including some wallowing buffalos. I see one black dolphin; the crew see a pink dolphin – a very rare sight – but, typically, I miss it.

At the village, we interview its leader, and Dr Branches takes us on his rounds. He talks to one of his patients, a fisherman with high mercury levels. He certainly has trouble walking properly. We are followed everywhere by crowds of children; all of them possess beautiful smiles. Dr Branches gives them balloons in return for taking hair samples, which he can check later for mercury levels. I am pleased with the shots we get of village life – some children acting as budding Peles; someone swinging in a hammock; women washing clothes in the river and then, of course, some incredible sunset shots. It all takes ages. Television is such an all-consuming monster of time and energy.

By now, our boatman is panicking as it is already twilight and, sure enough, the last leg of our journey takes place in virtual darkness. We have a fantastic view of the stars, the Milky Way and a satellite passing overhead. On the banks of the river we see the occasional flickering light in the bush. We pass by the tiny boat of a lone fisherman waiting for a prized catch. Bliss.

MERCURY POISONING VICTIM

Dr Branches arrives and takes us to see one of his patients, Emmanuel. He is 69 and the Doctor tells us he is in a bad way because of mercury poisoning. Emmanuel looks much older and cannot walk without help and constantly dribbles the odd speck of spittle. He is unable to talk much. He is no longer shaking because he has had treatment, but his brain has been irreversibly damaged. Dr Branches tells us Emmanuel has acquired the high level of mercury contamination because he lives above a gold shop.

When we come back with Julian Pettifer to film, it is again very depressing. Emmanuel looks a pathetic shell on camera and we get a moving interview from his daughter, bemoaning his plight.

CREPURIZAO

The flight from Itaituba lasts one hour and on the way we can see the Trans-Amazonian dirt road and the mighty Tapajos. As we progress into the interior, we soon see the mess the garimpeiros are making. By this stage, the terrain is becoming more hilly and the virgin forest stretches until the far horizon, apart from the odd pocket of garimpeiro intrusion. Suddenly we are at Crepurizao, a tottering array of shacks on stilts by the muddy waters of the river Crepurizao. There are two runways; one belongs to a rival air company and the other is the public runway, a small steep track of brown earth where we land. By garimpeiro standards, this is luxurious, but it is still scary nevertheless. Around the track, about 15 Cessna planes are housed in flimsy sheds. Several planes are also landing while we are disembarking. We have to be careful not to get run over as they dance in. On a typical day more than 30 planes come and go in daylight hours. And they say the boom time is starting to wane.

We are met by a contact in a huge truck which negotiates the massive potholes in the dirt track to the village with aplomb. Then we see what is optimistically called the high street. This is like going back to the days of Wyatt Earp and the Wild West. There are primitive buildings, running sewers and rubbish everywhere. Just about everyone around looks like a shifty outlaw. The shanty town – to our surprise – contains some well-stocked shops, so there is obviously money around. Several stores specialise in gold-mining equipment such as generators, engines, suction hoses, prospecting pans etc.

We are stared at by all and sundry as we drive down the street in style to the river front. Dozens of empty barrels and petrol cans are strewn across the track and an assortment of empty bottles laps onto the shore. About half a dozen small motor boats, the same type as carried us to Brasilia Legal, are stocking up with supplies for the dredgers and barges upriver. The river itself is filthy, all churned up because of the destruction of the banks. I am amazed to discover the locals can still manage to catch fish here.

The water level is low so many rocks are exposed and, as we chug upstream, our boat catches the top of the rocks with a horrible grating sound. The boatman is unperturbed and is an excellent navigator, weaving in and out of what must be rapids in the rainy season. The jungle itself is spectacular – high trees of different shapes and sizes, all dense and mysterious. The boatman tells us that wild cats such as lynx live here, as well as countless types of monkeys, though we see no sign of them. We do, however, see an array of brightly coloured birds, some with yellow crests. By the river banks are some rudimentary shelters surrounded by more rubbish and odd bits of mining equipment.

We stop about a mile upstream on a bend with a wide sand bank. Here is a dredger owned by a formidable woman called Madame Chance, who is supervising her boys working on the rickety vessel. We are invited aboard and see at last how they get gold up from the river. The barge has three engines which constantly pump up material from the river bed; this runs out over sluices lined with carpets. Every twenty four hours or so, they stop the pumps and scrape off the alluvial mixture stuck to the carpets. They then mix this material with mercury in a panning dish and the gold is separated.

I assume the suction pumps are controlled from the dredger or even the banks, but I am totally wrong. I notice that there are five big plastic water containers bobbing around near the boat with ropes going from them down into the murky depths. Each of the ropes marks where a diver is toiling eighteen feet down in pitch darkness, moving the hose of the pump around on the river bed. His only lifeline is a very precarious air-pipe. It is mind-boggling. One of the men on board tugs on a rope so a diver can come up to talk to us. A minute later, his head appears through the surface of the water; he is wearing a mask, a tatty diving suit and is very skinny. He blows hard, takes off his mask and somehow manages to grin. He and his fellow divers spend up to five hours at a time in these treacherous depths – all to scoop out around a hundred grammes of gold a day between them, worth around a thousand dollars.

Madame Chance, the owner, looks on approvingly, but we can imagine how tough she will be if her divers let her down. We arrange to come back and film here and then set off upstream again. We pass a variety of ingenious, Heath Robinson mining machines. Some are merely simple suction hoses with one engine, while others are large dredgers. We even see one low-tech team attacking the bank with a high pressure hose. Further up river, the rocks disappear and we are able to make a fast speed, leaning over like motor-bike passengers driving round bends in the road. We continue our odyssey and see the biggest dredger so far. It is something of a monster, with a suction hose attached to a crane. The vessel lurches in a terrifying way as the drill tears into the bank in a frantic search for gold.

The garimpeiros live on board; hammocks stretch between collapsing pieces of wood. The drinking water is kept in a plastic can – needless to say we stick to the water we have brought with us. We are well-covered up from the sun and mosquitoes. The worst time for these dangerous pests is in February, when many people die from malaria. There is also a big risk of hepatitis. I am not surprised, having seen the river water they are drinking. Looking around the craft, I am amused by a tiny wooden rack which holds the tooth brushes of the garimpeiros.

Home sweet home. One of the makeshift dredgers near Crepurizao

On the return journey we make faster progress as it is downstream, but we nearly come to grief when we just miss a low-lying rock while racing along at full speed. Back at what passes for a landing quay, we head for a much-needed beer. On our quest we gasp in astonishment at some shops with some great hunks of meat dangling from hooks and under attack from flies. There is some very dark meat on offer and I dread to think what it might be. The pilot has directed us to what he laughingly calls 'the best restaurant in town'; dilapidated tables and chairs are everywhere, but the food is doled out in huge portions by a grubby waiter carrying lumps of cooked meat on skewers. We stick resolutely to a beer.

We are keen to return to film later on another trip, but we realise with some trepidation that when we come back we will have to spend the night, as filming will take at least two days. We find the leader of the shanty town, who tells us there is indeed a hotel in the main street. It looks grim from the outside to say the least, but it looks like that will be our only choice.

Then it is time for us to go back to find our plane. We have to wait for a few passengers to arrive from far-flung gold areas or garimpos who have radioed in saying they will be delayed. There is, of course, no proper air traffic control – just a man seemingly with no training directing operations on an intermittent radio. While we are waiting, our pilot, David, tells us some hair-raising tales about travelling round this part of the Amazon. His brother once crash-landed on the top of the forest canopy and somehow managed to walk for eleven days before reaching the Tapajos and finding safety. Many other planes, especially in the early days of the boom, simply disappeared in the vast expanse of forest.

David tells us he is descended from a group of confederates who fled America in 1865 and tried to establish a slave colony in Santarém – now I realise why he has a Western name. He is proud of his ancestry and his experience and qualifications. He has only been prevented from a successful commercial airline career because he comes from northern Brazil. He tells us that to get into the state airline, Varig, you have to know the right people or be related to them, so he is doomed to flying six times a week from Santarém to Crepurizao via Itaituba. His plight has something of a universal theme: a man with standards battling to keep them, while all around are flouting them. David says he runs five miles a day and keeps fit, neither smoking or drinking. And for what? Probably one day to be hit by a drunken, unqualified garimpeiro pilot as he is taking off from this steep shale track that passes for a runway. I have to admire David, but feel subdued that such skill and endeavours are going to waste.

We prepare to take off but are stopped at the last minute. We have to wait for a garimpeiro who is suffering from gunshot wounds. He needs to be taken to hospital urgently in Itaituba. The pilot shrugs; a common occurrence, he says. The injured man finally arrives. He looks in a very bad way; he has a big wound in his chest which has been sewn up inexpertly. Slumped at the back of the plane, he clutches a drip into which blood is draining. A friend fans his face as we are able to take off to travel to what we regard as the height of civilisation – Itaituba.

When we return a couple of weeks later to Crepurizao for filming, we go straight to the decrepit hotel we checked out before. Inside it is not quite as bad as we feared. There are individual rooms, some even with a basic toilet and shower. Somehow this wooden edifice is still standing, with bare light bulbs trying desperately to illuminate a gloomy corridor. I keep expecting the whole building to topple over. My room is small and has an open window, through which I fear will fly swarms of mosquitoes. I put up a net I have brought with me over my bed. I am getting quite tense by now; everything is taking so long. We have lunch at the only clean place in town. There are platefuls of spaghetti and all kinds of meat joints on skewers and then endless supplies of stew, tomatoes, rice, and beans. We can hardly move afterwards.

In the afternoon we simply film life on the high street. The local sheriff is our guide; he tells us that a few months previously there were often shootings here causing a number of deaths, but life is now beginning to calm down a bit. We also interview the elected leader of the place, who says the government has abandoned them all and they are being treated as a long-lost indigenous and unruly tribe. We also film a couple of pieces to camera down by the harbour, where strange, straggly dogs gnaw at cattle bones. In a bar, we meet some of the divers on Madame Chance's dredger who we came across during our recce. They agree to let us film them having an allegedly good time gambling and chasing women. They also tell us the sad story of an Indian diver who died yesterday; his neck was broken when a sand bank collapsed on top of him. Chastened, we eventually creep to our matchwood hostel. I climb gingerly into my mosquito net and somehow get a reasonable night's sleep.

A typical garimpeiro panning for gold

The next day we film again by the river and get soaked when the heavens open. We retreat to a café. The waitresses move languidly around, provocatively brushing past me and the others. The women around here never stop hustling. We are pleased that our time in Crepurizao is nearly finished. At the airstrip, around twenty planes are waiting to take off. The runway is caked in mud and one group has to get out and push as the plane wheels become stuck. This time we are in a proper plane but there is no shortage of drama. On board with us are a drunk, two little pigs and a woman with malaria who is nine months pregnant, and in agony. An ambulance is summoned to meet her when we land.

RATO

As part of our research, Jan rings up an air taxi firm called Flipper, owned by a man named Ivo Lubrinna. He has been recommended as being both an astute garimpeiro leader and a local secretary of environment and mining. That means he is a poacher and gamekeeper all in one – sounds like someone we should meet. The company flies to Rato – a place we have been warned off because it is so dire and full of insects. The main drawback to Flipper is that the only plane it operates is a single engine Piper. We swallow hard, fully aware of the many tragedies involving planes with one engine.

The pilot is an Argentine who has become a naturalised Brazilian. He has been flying for 33 years (a plus), but becomes very animated and hot-headed when talking about Argentine politics (a minus). The departure time of the plane is left very vague when we buy two tickets at the Flipper office in Itaituba. Both Jan and I are weighed for safety reasons and to determine the price of the ticket. We pay for the tickets with money changed at the rather grand modern offices of the Banco do Brasil. Even here, though, some of the wildcat frontier spirit reigns. We cannot change travellers' cheques and only manage to exchange dollars "under the counter." No receipts are forthcoming and there is no record of any transaction at all.

Before leaving for Rato, we go back to the hotel to change into heavy-duty survival gear: thick shirts and armbands doused in DEET to ward off mosquitos. A car from the company picks us up and off we go. I like the informal nature of this place. Already a lot of people know us and many of them are helpful. I am amazed when some sunglasses I left in another local airline office have been delivered to our hotel. The Piper plane flying to Rato looks safe enough, but what about the condition of the engine beneath the cowling, I ask myself? While waiting, we talk to a scrawny woman who is going to the garimpo to see her husband. She is very worried about him because of the young teenage girls who turn up there and hope to have an easy life by living off men and getting up late. The reality is very different: the woman tells us disturbing stories of beatings and even murders of these underage girls. Life is very precarious and fragile in the garimpos. Many die from disease and violence, so it is easy to take on the attitudes that must have prevailed in Victorian times. It makes you fatalistic and expectant of bad news and death.

There are no seats in the Piper. I have to squat on a box in the co-pilot's position, desperately anxious to avoid touching the steering lever or the aerilon pedals by mistake, causing us to descend into the unwelcoming jungle below. There are no safety belts apart from one worn by the pilot, who fortunately has now calmed down and is talking about the river Tapajos instead of the Malvinas or military junta. The view from the plane is fantastic and we fool ourselves into thinking that perhaps it is worth the risk. We fly at about 2,000 feet and can peer right down in the forest, spotting the occasional track and remote landing strip. Some of these makeshift runways have no habitation around them at all. Possibly they are used solely by drug-runners and other unsavoury characters. We can see the winding course of the Tapajos for miles ahead.

South of Itaituba, the river changes its character dramatically, becoming narrower, with many rocks, rapids and bends. After 45 minutes hurtling through space at around 140 miles an hour, we spot the settlement of Rato. The runway is a tiny clearing in the forest near a small muddy river. The landing is perfect and we taxi up to the most dilapidated and unsuitable terminal building I have ever seen. It is basically a lean-to and reminds me of the trading posts featured in Hollywood westerns. At any moment, I expect ruthless trappers to barge in carrying bearskins and captured Indian women. On display on the decrepit shelves are the basics of jungle life – maize, flour, rice. All of these staples are distributed free to the sorry crowd of around 5,000 inhabitants who have to live in this hostile area. But they have to pay for other necessities, such as batteries and whisky.

The lord of this architectural masterpiece is Ivo Lubrinna himself. Despite the harsh surroundings, he still gives off something of the image of a successful businessman. He is wearing a smart white shirt and expensive-looking sunglasses. His desk in the corner of this terminal shack is neat and tidy, with an electronic calculator, which looks completely out of place. Ivo is hunched over the radio bellowing orders when we walk in. He is very friendly and gives both Jan and me a vice-type squeeze on the arm in greeting.

Ivo gets one of his henchmen to take us upriver to see his local village. On the way, he shows us two monkeys chained up alongside the arrivals hut. For some reason, the female monkey hates the local women and apparently hurls herself at them whenever they approach. The monkey makes no fuss about Jan – presumably European women are OK – but then a downtrodden garimpo woman appears and the monkey goes absolutely berserk.

The boat is very long and lurches high in the water. It is tremendous fun zooming fast round the bends surrounded by high trees, behind which strange animal noises waft towards us. The henchman takes us to the sorry village, where more meagre stores are gathered outside on a base of sand. Just about every dwelling seems to be some kind of store, with the same provisions of tinned milk, cokes, beer and a vast assortment of tablets.

We return to the staging post where Ivo joins us and heaves his massive frame into the long boat. We only have to cross to the other bank this time and he sets off down a forest trail brandishing a big stick. The path leads to another sand bank where there are even flimsier dwellings; they are basically tents with blue sheeting over them, and are exposed to the air at the sides. Pots and pans are stacked neatly on wobbly shelving and we are invited in for a hot coffee from a thermos flask. This is Ivo's field HQ and is kept remarkably tidy, despite the appearance of chaos.

As he swallows copious quantities of coffee, milk and water, Ivo delivers a passionate soliloquy about the state of the garimpos and the mercury issue. He says people like him have been abandoned by the federal authorities. He rails against academics, doctors and scientists, saying they have not researched the mercury question properly and have created a Tower of Babel as they refuse to talk to each other and do not share their research. He castigates bank-owners for not doing enough to deliver cheap retorts into the area – vital equipment for heating up alluvial material and separating the gold by the use of mercury.

By now, Ivo's pristine white shirt is covered in streams of sweat. His eyes are bulging, his belly is trembling and his eyes revolve manically as he continues his tirade against colonial powers and politicians. It is all highly entertaining and full of common sense. He then takes us to see his men. We have to stagger along a muddy track, often balancing on sticks to stop us being soaked by the many puddles – now I know why he gave us the sticks. We emerge from bushes to gaze at a massive hole in the forest. About 20 feet down, teams of men are toiling away with drilling machines, pumping up material they hope contains that elusive gold. It is devastation on a huge scale, all in the domain of the local government official responsible for the environment. Banks have been eroded, trees felled and ugly piles of mud ooze everywhere.

One extra-large headache for our local hero of the environment is that most of the soil has been washed downstream; it will be impossible for him to make good the land as he claims he wants to. He will have to dig as big a hole elsewhere just to fill in this one and, of course, there are no bulldozers and mechanical diggers around to make it happen anyway. It is a primeval scene with a gaggle of under-nourished garimpeiros coming up to report to him on their progress. Their legs are stained with dirt, their bare feet squelching in the mud but their eyes remain filled with a lust for gold. They only stop this scrambling in the earth when Brazil plays a football match and they are allowed to watch a television driven by battery power.

While we stand talking to Ivo about the economic and managerial skills needed to run a garimpo, we hear a warning shout. About ten metres from us, a large section of the bank slides into the morass below – we are nearly swept along with it. If the faulty planes or ferocious insects don't get you, then this environmental holocaust will. We return to the airfield to see our volatile Argentine pilot strumming the propeller. He is anxious to take off while there is still enough light to get back. We are joined on the journey by three garimpeiros; I am sure there is too much weight on the plane so we all have to lean forward to help the plane take off before we plunge into the jungle. All is well until I shift my position to try to peer in the forest below, spooking my fellow passengers. I suppose they are terrified that this big, crazy Englishman will send the plane into a tailspin.

Soon we are safely back in Itaituba. It seems like a huge metropolis compared to Rato. We go back to our hotel and try to get some rest. Around 10pm there is always a violent kung-fu film – not surprising given the Brazilian machismo which is on full display here. I am woken around 2am by an almighty clap of thunder. The whole hotel seems to vibrate and then shake in the wind as torrents of rain lash against the walls. Water starts pouring into my room through a hole in the roof, but fortunately not onto my bed. The storms come and go for quite a while; it is very exhilarating.

When we return to film in Rato, we manage to procure a twin-engined plane to fly us there. But this plane also does not have any seats. We have another passenger with us – a man from a telephone company who is going to upgrade the network in Rato – so we are incredibly cramped. The heavy camera tri-pod is draped over our legs and we are sitting on each other's feet, all hunched up, hot and frightened.

Mercifully, the trip is shorter than last time – only about 35 minutes. But it is more bumpy and we all feel sick, especially Adrian Cooper, the cameraman, who is trying to film from the front seat. His insides lurch violently when the plane banks steeply just as he is looking intently through the camera eyepiece.

All aboard. Our intrepid crew squash into one of those terrifying small planes in the Amazon jungle.

When we land I have to drag myself out of the plane as my foot has gone to sleep. I cannot move for several minutes. Other members of the team also limp around for a while. We are like a group of crippled performing seals. We then meet Ivo again at his store and wait while Adrian overcomes his nausea. Ivo enters into the spirit of filming with gusto. He dons a kind of pith helmet he was given in South Africa five years ago. It makes him look like something out of the nineteenth century, a colonialist on the march. We film some amazing scenes of him sitting imperiously in his long boat and striding around his kingdom, complete with sticks and helmet. The interview with him goes really well and then we film some scenes in the mining hole Ivo took us to last time.

I clamber down with Adrian and Heron, the sound man, as I want to take some photos. It is very hot, wet and dangerous. The noise of the motors whining is deafening. Around us, a few garimpeiros aim their hoses at the bottom of precarious sandbanks. Heron asks one what will happen if the bank collapses.

"Then I'm dead," comes the matter of fact reply.

Not surprisingly, we do not linger long at this scene out of bedlam. Everywhere there are pounding noises, toxic smells, dejected and resigned faces, with the miners spending 13 hours a day scrabbling for gold. They will be paid about a gramme of gold a day, or about ten dollars. They will spend most of it on drink or on the various women dotted around the place.

Like the men, the women are depressing here. We see one with a huge gold chain round her neck and another whose face is riddled with pox. There is another dressed in a kind of purple trouser suit with several gold teeth, who tries to charm us away into the forest for a few minutes of so-called pleasure. She is not that bad looking, but we have no problems resisting her advances. Some of the other women are fat, old and incredibly rough.

Then we have to rush back to the plane, and again all lean forward as we lumber to take off. What a day. In spite of everything, we like Ivo – perhaps a bit of a rogue, yes,

Our sweaty team takes a breather with Ivo Lubrinna and his workers

but doing a difficult job and controlling his men reasonably fairly. The most abiding memory I will take away of him is when he ordered his men to build a bridge with tree trunks across a stream of muddy water to try to keep him clean.

"There," he said, turning to Julian. "That's why I stay here. It's the only place in Brazil a black man like me can give an order which is instantly obeyed."

The trip back is another example of Dante-like chaos. By this stage, the whole plane stinks like an off-colour sauna and we are all dripping with sweat. We all have a good laugh at our ridiculous situation, especially when I announce some on-board safety regulations as if we are on a reputable international flight.

Julian Pettifer meets Ivo Lubrinna in his kingdom of gold

SANTARÉM

While based here, we set off early one day and take some great shots at the market by the water front. There are vultures and pigs eating fish by the river. On the market stalls, chickens, lotions and potions are on sale amid a seething mass of Amazonian life. We then meet some people from the Group for the Defence of the Amazon. They are open, positive and cheery – a stark contrast to the shifty, suspicious faces we have seen at Crepurizao and other garimpos. It is a treat too to see women who are not whores but have sparkle and grace. We are greatly impressed by a street drama they perform; they act out various scenes of a fisherman getting mercury poisoning and dying. The final scene is a trial in which the fisherman is found guilty. After all, he is culpable for eating the poisoned fish, a true parable of Amazonian life where the victim is not protected and blamed for the ills of society.

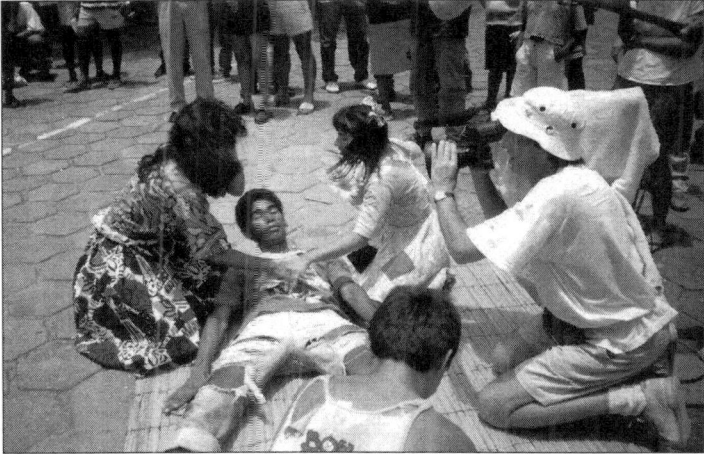

Capturing the drama of a fisherman struck down by mercury poisoning

MANAUS

During the five week trip to Brazil, I have the chance to spend a while in Manaus, a city deep in the Amazon jungle. I am writing this entry while in the airport lounge at Santarém, but am finding it hard going. All kinds of winged insects keep landing on me and on the computer keyboard. It is time to leave. The plane to Manaus is quite crowded and it feels threatening – I don't know why; maybe it dawns on me tonight just how fragile you are to be flying in darkness, 33,000 feet above nothingness and potential oblivion. Before landing I can see Manaus, which looks a huge city from the air. What is a place like this doing so deep into the Amazon jungle? The airport also appears to be massive, certainly in comparison to the little shacks that pass for airport terminals in the garimpos.

The airport is around 12 miles out of town and the road into the centre is built up all the way. It feels more like America, with bars, restaurants, and garages (or should I say 'gas stations'). They have all sprung up here because of the free port status of Manaus, so I feel as though I am back in the first world. Well, nearly, but not quite. My cab suddenly develops a transmission problem so we lurch and judder along pathetically. At one point, the driver has to stop and fiddle around with jump leads. The road is dark so I worry about being mugged. After lots of cursing and heaving, the driver gets the car moving again but the trip is something of a nightmare. The driver has to keep his speed up to prevent stalling and so we tear at breakneck speed down crowded streets, crossing red lights and busy junctions. I am very glad to get to the hotel, which is right in the middle of the city. Immediately, I go to look at one of the sights of Manaus, the Opera House. It is a very imposing beautiful building, a long way from the garimpos.

Back at the hotel, I think I hear a mosquito in the night, so I shove on more repellent and sleep in my trousers with my socks tucked in. I also keep the air-conditioning going. It makes a tremendous racket, but it's worth it. In the morning, I go for a walk on to the floating dock. It is very, very hot – even at 8am. The port is busy, with a couple of big ocean-going ships unloading containers. Incredibly, it is nearly a thousand miles to the sea from here. Dozens of big river boats complete with swaying hammocks on deck compete for passengers. Sadly, I do not have enough time to go to the nearby meeting of the waters between the dark-coloured Negro River and the sandy coloured Amazon. Instead, I just wander around the busy arcades selling electrical goods and wander past pleasant parks and relics of colonial architecture. The Opera House in daylight is truly stunning. Whoever built it must have had great vision and determination.

After strolling around bathed in sweat, I take a cab to look at the local research centre in the rainforest. Again, I have a loony cab-driver, tooting a warning on his horn to other drivers that he is hurtling past them on the outside or occasionally the inside. Manaus is truly huge. You would never guess you are so deep into the Amazon interior.

The research centre is disappointing. The only thing I manage to see is a peixe-boi, or sea cow, swimming around in a tank. It seems to have few cares in the world. We just evade a tropical downpour on our slalom back to the hotel. The drive back to the airport is also very hair-raising, with another frustrated driver gesticulating wildly at everyone. Every so often, street hawkers selling strawberries, newspapers and even Brazilian flags accost our vehicle. I am certainly glad to escape this menagerie by arriving at the airport.

CRISTALINO RIVER

At crack of dawn, we set off for the Cristalino River near Alta Floresta. We are joined in our van by an American couple in late middle age, who turn out to be tour operators for the elderly. They are great fun and avid bird-watchers.

During the journey there is the occasional shriek of delight as one of them spots a different kind of Amazonian bird. At the Teles Pires River we decant into a small boat which becomes heavily laden with our bodies and equipment. I am shocked by the state of the river, a filthy brown colour with lumps of detergent and oil streaks everywhere. The junction with the aptly named Cristalino is striking. Clear water is draining into an amalgam of gunge. We spend some time filming this merging of the waters. It will make a great symbolic image near the start of our film. As we sail up the Cristalino, it is like entering paradise. The forest and waters are pristine. We spot a capivara standing by the river edge – it is a huge rodent, the size of a small pig. The creature has a long face and watches us intently for a few minutes before shuffling off in the bush.

There are more delights to come. By now, the American twitchers are in nirvana. We spot a wide variety of birds, from dazzling blue kingfishers to striking yellow and blue parrots to white herons. We find a lodge in an idyllic place in a clearing, a marvellous oasis of tranquillity. We go further upstream and Julian films a piece to camera where he talks about how this paradise has been affected by mercury, the stuff of the gods. We film some rapids and then get some incredible close up shots of sunlight streaking into the forest and casting shadows on bright green leaves. Brown and yellow butterflies on the sandy bank are also expertly filmed in large close up by Adrian.

Lunch is a very humble affair, with caipirinhas (rum, lime and sugar), beer and a delicious mixture of chicken, beans, rice and pineapple. It is very hard to get moving after such a meal. Jan goes to sleep in a hammock. Eventually, we get going again and have another treat: we spot four tapirs basking by the river side, truly mesmerising creatures with long snouts and knowing stares. Our trip to paradise has been very worthwhile for its filmic and spiritual uplift.

Back in the van we stop to film a different scene as we come across the tangled aftermath of tree burning to clear the way for development. Blackened stumps are twisted into hideous shapes. Why they have to burn this beautiful forest is a bit of a mystery to me. It seems so uneconomic to sell the timber on such a small scale and the soil produced is so poor, even for the scrawny cattle which will graze here. It is a sad and pathetic spectacle. Julian does a highly polished piece to camera, walking along a long tree trunk. Once again, we have been reminded of the contradictions of the mighty Amazonian rivers and forests. They are majestic natural wonders but are increasingly blighted and changed by the rapacious greed of human beings.

CHAPTER TEN

The Psychotic Border

I have been on two trips to South Korea during my lifetime. One was in late 1993 on a filming assignment for the BBC; the other time was in late 2011 to visit my elder son, Phil, who was teaching English near Seoul. Although the country had obviously become more modern during this period, one issue facing the country has been stubbornly impervious to change. Despite the best efforts of the international community, North Korea has remained a defiant threat – a reclusive, hard-line communist state armed with nuclear weapons. Having seen the collapse of the Berlin Wall, I have been hoping to see the demise of the totalitarian regime in North Korea and a subsequent peaceful reunification with South Korea. However, it seems I will have to be patient a while longer. This seems to be one ideological tectonic plate which has become firmly stuck.

On both my trips, I could not help but marvel at the efficient development of South Korea. It is a rich nation which is proud of its values and has been part of the growing prosperity in East Asia. I shared my BBC assignment to Seoul in 1993 with the reporter Julian Pettifer. He had visited the city previously as a young man in the mid-1950s and he could not believe how such a modern, shimmering city of more than ten million people had risen out of nowhere. We had been sent to South Korea to make a short film for a New Year programme focusing on some of the potential flashpoints at the time. The Cold War – bizarrely – was still in full swing on the Korean peninsula and our mission was to travel to the border to assess the risks for the future.

While we wandered, awestruck, around the new impressive skyscrapers in Seoul, we could not help but think about the vulnerability of the city. It is only 35 miles from the border, no distance at all for North Korean missiles. During our trip we made contact with the American forces stationed in the area and were taken to witness some of their manoeuvres. All I can remember is being frozen as we filmed young men leaping in and out of fox holes in the bitter December weather.

The highlight of our trip was a visit to the Demilitarised Zone (DMZ), a buffer zone on the border where more than a million armed men faced one another. It was hard to comprehend that such grotesque posturing has been in place for 40 years, with most of the aspiring combatants from the same country. A description of our crazy day out at the frontier follows.

* * *

As we drive along the highway from Seoul to the frontier with North Korea, I have a tremendous sense of expectancy. My impressions of this uneasy border have been framed only by brief glimpses of the settlement of Panmunjom on television. But as I knew only too well, on the ground you can always soak in much more and I cannot wait to see such a unique place. About an hour out of Seoul, we come across the first of many check-points. At the beginning, they are manned only by police. As we grow closer to the border, the military are much more in evidence.

We have to negotiate a crossing at Imjin bridge, which was totally destroyed in the Korean War forty years previously. Only a few stubs of concrete and mangled wire remain, and what is left of the nearby railway bridge has been turned into a crossing for road traffic. A procession of military trucks trundles up and down here, causing significant delays. However, there are also a number of tourist buses bringing crowds of inquisitive South Koreans and Japanese on their way to peer across the border into the antiquated, apparently misguided world of North Korea. What a strange combination – military might and tourist curiosity. This bewildering amalgam is well in evidence in a service area near the bridge. Here you can buy cokes, puppets in striking national costume, and engraved plates. It is an incongruous shopping display as one prepares to enter a potential war zone and one of the most heavily armed corners of the world.

Outside the cocoon of tourist support systems, there is another stark reminder of the military backdrop to the journey. Dotted over a large area are relics of the fighting from the early fifties – tank shells, warplanes, and artillery pieces laid out neatly like children's toys. There is even a rickety railway carriage from the days you could take the train up beyond the 38th parallel, which now forms the military demarcation line. Hidden away in the midst of this museum are several stone monuments, honouring the dead and celebrating the fruits of victory and independence. The South Koreans are understandably partial to this type of monument; they have a lot to remember and commemorate. Yet by now I already feel I have seen enough of them. I have been especially perturbed by some monuments on display at the Independence Hall of Korea, two hours south of Seoul. These exude an edgy national chauvinism, mirroring the monuments I have seen in the idealised Park of Achievement opposite the Cosmos hotel in Moscow during my stay there in 1990. In mitigation, I suppose some of these Korean monuments have been built during the twilight days of the authoritarian regimes in South Korea in the eighties, which now – mercifully – have disappeared.

After we have waited in line to cross the single file bridge, I sense we are now really entering border territory. Both sides of the river are lined by ugly fencing and barbed wire. Ahead, I know the place will be swarming with hundreds of thousands of troops – so what I see now is merely the aperitif. Bizarrely, the scene also has its beauty. Ice glistens on the waters of the river and geese squawk overhead while elegantly flying in their mid-winter wanderings. The main road winds its way past a seemingly endless series of military barracks, each with a sandy football pitch by the entrance. Even amid such military might, the human spirit still needs time to play. In summer, much of this area must be delightful, with its rolling hills and numerous trees. Today in the watery winter sun, everything has a dull brown hue.

After about a quarter of an hour, we arrive at Camp Bonifas, named after one of the US officers who was axed to death by enraged North Koreans in 1976. We decant from our minibus into a hall where one of the fastest talkers in the world, a US Army corporal, gives us a rat-a-tat briefing. Despite his catatonic delivery, the content is absorbing. He gives us tit-bits of information about the North Korean leader, Kim Il Sung, and an authoritative account of how the infamous axe murders took place. This is still a touchy subject and the incident clearly shows how in the DMZ there are rules which are broken at everyone's peril. Under the veneer of civilisation, this is a place of hatred where raw emotions are kept in check only by rigid procedures, and advance planning is vital for anything out of the ordinary, so as not to scare the other side.

The axe murders happened near a UN control post on the Bridge of No Return, which we can see from the top of the hill we are on. At the time of the killings, some US troops had been pruning some trees to aid visibility, but the North Koreans were disturbed by this break to the routine. They stormed across the bridge to demand that the activity cease. In the ensuing melee, two US servicemen, including Captain Bonifas, were hacked to death. They were terrifying killings, which explains the present day twitchiness of all the officials who escort us round the area.

We are told when entering the Pagoda Peace Towers and other observation points on the Military Demarcation Line not to make sudden, unusual hand gestures, which can be interpreted as provocative or hostile. Even in this demilitarised zone, there is still a rapid deployment guard of military police on alert to deal with emergencies. One such incident happened when a Soviet defector escaped into the UN side of the Joint Security Area pursued by North Koreans. In other words, this place is a constant tinderbox waiting to go up. Despite this, as an outsider, I find it hard to understand the tension.

Our American PR escort is nervous throughout our stay, especially as we want to depart from the normal media tour routine by visiting the Swiss neutral area. I never realised that such a strange piece of territory exists on the earth. The Swiss, along with the Swedes, have been asked by the UN to act for the Americans and South Koreans as neutral officials after the war and to supervise the armistice. On the other side, Poland and Czechoslovakia have been asked to do the same. However, after the break-up of Czechoslovakia about a year before our visit, the North Koreans asked the Czech delegation to leave, leaving the poor old Poles on their own to try to interpret the mysterious pronouncements of Kim Il Sung.

The Swiss delegation is led by Major General Bernard Sandoz, a figure resplendent in a smart grey uniform with masses of gold braid on his cap. He is tall, erect and magnificent in his military coat, bedecked in black gloves and an immaculately coiffeured beard. He is an intellectual and civilised man in his mid-fifties, who somehow has to try to make sense and bring order to the Alice in Wonderland world he inhabits. He clearly relishes his independence and neutrality, and is a contrast to the nervy American minders at Camp Bonifas. He is not the strong silent type, however, and never stops talking, explaining in minute detail all the precise and intricate procedures of the area.

The Major General regards his patch as his own kingdom, refusing to stop at the UN/US checkpoints. Everywhere is deserted as we wend our way through the undulating countryside, with its icy fields and brown trees. It all seems so innocent and peaceful. The only intruders are geese and galloping pheasants, gleefully pointed out by the verbose Major General. Eventually, we arrive at his camp, an oasis of civilisation and sanity in the midst of this crazy diplomatic and military stand-off.

His camp consists of a few red-painted log cabins perched on a hill and surrounded by trees. It seems more like a mountain retreat at the foot of the Alps and it is hard to remember that these innocent buildings are situated only yards from a barbed wire fence marking the actual border. The HQ is cosy and warm, with a bar and other trappings of humanity – all this only feet away from territory belonging to an unstable dictator.

The Major General is determined to whip us into shape and gives us a full briefing for the next couple of hours. He introduces us to his Swedish counterpart, who is playing host to a group of children from a nearby South Korean village in the DMZ. It is nearly Christmas after all and everyone here seems determined to celebrate the season of peace and goodwill, despite the current corrosive tension over North Korea's nuclear programme. We set up our camera on the order of the Major General and wait for the show to unfold.

A group of about twenty children with animated faces is dressed in national costume in lavish shades of orange, yellow and purple with long-flowing robes. They are seemingly oblivious to the obscene array of military hardware pitted against each other on the boundaries of the DMZ just over a mile away. What a mad world. These children may be at serious risk at any time from a military strike but are content to do what kids do all over the world at Christmas, charming an adult audience by singing carols and celebrating the joy and innocence of life. The children sing, dance, play drums and captivate everyone.

After the concert we have to break off and rush to the Peace Pagoda Tower itself. Despite the special privileges that journalists can sometimes enjoy, we have to re-join a regular tour to go to the vantage point where we can see the North Korean positions. Everybody has to be protected by the military police and if we miss our rendezvous, that will be it. The North Koreans across the way are used to a certain routine and a group of journalists turning up at a different time might spread alarm. Sadly for us, the tour schedule leaves us little time for filming. The American serviceman with the machine gun patter is back again. He barks out some descriptions about what we can see from the pagoda. Immediately below are three Nissen-style huts where discussions and negotiations are held with North Korean officials. Beyond that is an imposing rectangular building on the North Korean side which looks like a museum.

We try desperately to film the North Korean guards, who are watching us through their binoculars. Their faces seem thinner, more angular than their South Korean counterparts, who stand defiantly in front of us to protect us. The malnourished appearance of the North

Koreans gives them a menacing air, or perhaps we are just demonising them in our minds. Our guards position themselves at the corners of the huts, showing half their bodies to the North Koreans, only 20 metres away at the other end of the buildings. Their posture enables them to draw a weapon easily if necessary and quickly take shelter.

We are then hustled into the negotiating hut, where contacts have been taking place until earlier in the year. All meetings were called off then because of tension over the North's nuclear programme. Inside, we can see a table with the flags of both sides on display. The gabbling US corporal explains how, in the past, there have been extensive arguments over the size of the flags used. At one stage, both sides tried hard to outdo each other by bringing in a bigger flag at subsequent meetings. Eventually, the flags became so big that they could not be carried into the building. Even the squabbling negotiators realised it was a complete farce and arranged an uneasy truce. However, even now we think the North Korean flag on display is bigger, but our verbally challenged corporal explains to us that the base of the UN flag is bigger, so honour appears to be satisfied.

The Swiss Major General is clearly bored by this set-piece routine for tourists, and yanks us into the armistice building next door. This appears to be where the real work goes on away from the histrionics and one-upmanship. It is in here that the neutral powers apparently try to knock some sense into the opposing powers. The Major General urges us to cross beyond the table into what is effectively North Korea. It is quite an adrenalin rush to step into one of the last rigid communist societies on earth.

We then walk with the Major General and the hapless American PR stooge towards a nearby observation point. Our US chaperone is clearly terrified, as our guards have disappeared. We are therefore just a small unprotected group, at the mercy of jumpy North Koreans a few metres away. The Major General treats the situation with disdain and nothing untoward happens. At the nearby official observation point, tourists are still milling around, so we wait for them to leave and then record some pieces to camera with Julian. Because we are transmitting this material in a few weeks' time, we have to ensure that Julian's words will not be out of date by the time the special show goes on air.

We have to move very fast and there is little time to take in what is going on in front of us. However, I do manage to glimpse some big loud-speakers near to us, which suddenly jerk into life, bombarding us with propaganda about the righteous ways of the North Korean regime. I also look down on the Bridge of No Return, where the axe murders happened. It was here that President Clinton had put the cat among the pigeons last July when he marched about 15 metres onto the bridge. What the twitchy North Korean guards made of such a flagrant departure from routine and protocol goodness only knows. From the observation post, all looks fairly tranquil with no obvious weaponry, but we know that just over the hill are the massed ranks of the main North Korean forces. On our left is the North Korean propaganda village. No-one lives there but the fetish over flags is in evidence again. Here the North Koreans have built a huge flag pole to dwarf the one on the South Korean side.

When we have finished filming, we walk back to safety. Once again, our American minder looks very uncomfortable and tries to hustle us along. I want to dawdle and savour these special moments at this weird place. We retreat to the security of the Major General's log cabin, where we tuck into pizza and Heineken beer. The Major General is still holding forth about his unusual kingdom until the moment we leave. As we get back into our van for the trip back to Seoul, we have to hand over some blue and white arm bands that have marked us out as press. Our lugubrious American minder observes that, without them, we definitely would have run a great risk of being shot. It is a sobering moment at the end of one of the most surreal days of my life and in the end I am relieved to be back on the road to the South Korean capital.

CHAPTER ELEVEN

The Land of the Rising Sun

I had always been intrigued by Japan, the Land of the Rising Sun. There was never a chance to go there while on *Newsnight*, but I did eventually travel to the country while working on a documentary for the *Assignment* documentary programme at the start of 1993. By this time, Japan had become an economic powerhouse, number two in the world behind the mighty America. It had been an incredible journey of change since starting to rebuild virtually from scratch after World War Two. Already, however, the Japanese miracle was running out of steam, with signs of the deflation which was to blight the country in the years that followed until the present day.

The idea for my documentary appeared simple on the surface – to explore why crime rates in Japan are so much lower than in the West. The Japanese claim this phenomenon results from a combination of loyalty to society and skilful community policing. They are especially proud of their Koban system, a network of tiny police sub-stations which nestle on numerous street corners in towns and cities. A policeman is known here as Omawarisan, or 'Mr Walkaround'. The presence of many of these

Omawarisans helps to keep offences to a minimum; crime figures for murder, attempted murder, and violent robbery were way beneath those in Britain for the same offences. However, such impressive low crime rates turned out to be only part of the true picture.

Some of Tokyo's finest Omawarisans on duty

Some critics of the system at the time said that it gave the Japanese police the ability to pry into every nook and cranny of their beats. They could engage in extensive surveillance and assemble a database of everyone's business. Their presence also carried with it a sense of intimidation. Gordon Brewer, the BBC Tokyo correspondent and my partner on this film, said that the police were not just out on the streets but were in people's heads. There was also extreme criminality in Japan in the form of the yakuza, Japan's answer to the Mafia, who ran all sorts of rackets linked to drugs, prostitution, gambling, and corrupt real estate deals.

The first problem when making this film was to gain access to a local police station, a prison, and a juvenile crime centre. The Japanese Justice Ministry was known to be notorious in its suspicion of the foreign press; it was hardly likely to fall over itself to help us. Fortunately, I had two formidable Japanese women as interpreters and fixers. They set to work with true Japanese zeal and bombarded the relevant PR officials with the requisite amount of threats, flattery, cajolery, cunning and downright bloody-mindedness

First into action was Fuyuko Nishisato. She comes from the northern island of Hokkaido, whose inhabitants are prone to scorn what they regard as the meek, centralising attitudes of the rest of Japan – good attitudes for a fixer in Japan. Fuyuko set up an initial meeting with several bureaucrats from the Justice Ministry for Gordon and me. The ministry was based in an uninspiring modern office block. It formed part of the administrative complex of government buildings in central Tokyo, not far from the Imperial Palace, one of the most valuable tracts of real estate in the world.

Our appointment was a bizarre encounter from start to finish. We were confronted by a posse of officials, who appeared rather nervous. One of them gestured us to the corner of an open plan office; it was time for the ritual exchange of meishi, or business cards. Without one of these, any foreign professional in Japan may as well turn tail for Narita Airport and catch the first flight home. No meishi, no identity.

Fuyuko then turned to me and asked me to make my opening comments. I had been in the country for less than 48 hours and was horribly jet-lagged after the 13 hour flight from Europe across the wastes of Siberia. I also had no real idea how to tackle the meeting, on which the project would stand or fall. I had a suspicion that at least a couple of the Japanese officials could speak English. The PR man was youthful and earnest. The junior bureaucrat was submissive and the man seemingly in charge was aloof and disdainful with a steely stare.

Out of the corner of my eye, I noticed there was another official in listening distance, who in fact must have been the most senior person in the room. He feigned disinterest, flicking through a number of television channels with a remote control, but I could tell that his ears were tuned to our conversation so he could exercise a veto if he thought his group was giving too much away. It was a rather inconclusive meeting, with much discussion about our motives, the problems filming in penal institutions and the impossibility of landing an interview with the justice minister. Occasionally, this non-meeting of minds was punctuated by the odd guffaw or sigh from the senior bureaucrat, who was still pretending to be absorbed in the television.

The list of requests now had to be followed up by another Japanese fixer, Chako Sugi-Bellamy. She was married to an eccentric Englishman, who built his own motorbikes. Chako occasionally threw off the image of dutiful Japanese wife and mother to ride pillion on her husband's bike and charge around at 150 miles an hour on motorways.

Both she and Fuyuko had a lot in common: both were in their forties; both had lived in England and had a rebellious streak. Both were workaholics but they could let their hair down, and enjoy glasses of hot sake and a feast of raw fish and noodles. More importantly, both were possessed with infinite patience and persistence, and carried the scalps of many Japanese bureaucrats.

Both were also used to working with crazy gaijin, the rather unflattering Japanese word for foreigners. They were used to people like me putting their foot in it, sometimes literally. For instance, I horrified both of them on several occasions by breaking a social taboo and forgetting to take off my shoes when going into a traditional restaurant or someone's house. The two women also knew how to cope with a foreigner's frustrations and temper tantrums when constantly running up against Nippon red tape. They knew how helpless gaijin could become when confronted by the complexities of travelling on the Tokyo underground or booking tickets on the bullet train.

I had first-hand experience of Fuyuko's talents when I travelled alone with her on a recce trip outside Tokyo. Our first destination was the town of Fukui to the north, not far from the Sea of Japan. The town is near a large concentration of nuclear power stations and is something of a doleful backwater. The purpose of the trip was to meet a hospital consultant with unusual talents. Dr Mitso Yoshimura had made his reputation by helping members of the yakuza to restore their missing little fingers, cut off as a sign of penance when failing their bosses. The tell-tale stumps on their hands meant it was difficult for them if they wanted to go straight and be accepted as a normal member of the community. To counter this, the good doctor had perfected a method of cutting off a toe and using it to replace the missing finger on the hand in an amazing feat of microsurgery. Fuyuko's dealings with him were incredibly efficient. Permission to film an operation was easily obtained, though, as the footage eventually showed, this was not a process for the squeamish.

After meeting the enterprising doctor, I was whisked off by Fuyuko to catch a train to the tip of the Wakayama peninsula in the south of Honshu, the main island in Japan. The surprising thing to me about the journey was how much mountainous terrain we passed through. My impression beforehand of Japan was of crowded islands with skyscrapers and little countryside to speak of. The reality is different: sixty per cent of Japan is remote and mountainous. Only on the coastal plains are the teeming population centres. On the way to Osaka, we saw countless paddy fields and Alpine-looking houses. Osaka itself was a disappointment – a huge sprawling settlement with little evidence of its historical roots. We had to change here to catch a smaller train on the twisting route south to the tip of Wakayama.

While waiting, I had my first glimpse of a Shinkansen, a bullet train. Its Japanese name has such a poetic ring, so it was disappointing to discover its functional meaning in Japanese: new trunk line. British Rail in all its former glory could hardly have come up with something worse. There was no disappointment, however, in its appearance, which oozed quiet, controlled power. The trip to Wakayama involved travelling for long stretches along a rocky coastline with some ravishing views of tiny fishing villages – again denting the clichéd picture of Japan. Katsura, our eventual destination after a three and a half hour leg, even had a Mediterranean feel to it. Even in February, there was enough sunshine to bring cheer to a jaded winter mien.

It is also a hot spring resort, a reminder that much of Japan lies above unstable fault lines. Several resort hotels have sprung up in the area, offering both indoor and outdoor naturally heated pools. Our hotel maintained the customs of a ryokan, a traditional Japanese inn. A gaijin is a rare sight here, as the place is an unashamed celebration of Japanese culture. The atmosphere is a mixture of informality and convention. You are supposed to wear the correct bath robe while walking round the hotel. The set times for meals are strictly adhered to, and it is frowned upon to stay in a room on your own.

After much persuasion, Fuyuko managed to secure two rooms for us. Mine was in traditional style, which entailed sleeping on the floor on a mattress. The baths used to be mixed but the Americans put paid to that after the occupation at the end of the Second World War. Fuyuko and I went our separate ways, though, given the decorous, relaxed ambience of the place, it would have seemed perfectly natural to have continued our conversations sitting naked in two feet of hot sulphuric water.

However, sexual activity is not high on the list at a ryokan, though it is rumoured that high-spirited groups of young people do break the segregation rule late at night. I was happy to be on my own in the outdoor bath. Although the weather was cold, it was quite a joy to sit in the warm water, staring up at a full moon and hearing the ocean a stone's throw away.

We were in Katsura to meet a reformed gangster, a former member of the yakuza. His name was Atzumo Yamamoto and he was taking refuge in a summer house belonging to a childhood friend. Yamamoto had served ten years in prison for a string of violent crimes, yet he was a firm believer in chivalry and manners. He castigated the new generation of Japanese gangsters, who he believed had strayed from the traditional concepts of honour and brotherly love, and had been ensnared by making money. In his view, they had exchanged a moral code for a credit card and sharp suit.

Yamamoto was so disgusted with the new breed of yakuza that he had decided to go straight three years ago. He lamented these declining standards of modern gangsters when we interviewed him at his hideaway.

He said: "In the past there was a purpose, whether it was fighting or whatever, but now they do not have any intention of leading a hard life, nor do they have any will to study the ethics of the yakuza. This is what earning money has reduced them to."

He was also angry that the new yuppie yakuza had abandoned the concepts of giri and ninjo – classic Japanese tenets of weighing individual duty with the greater good of the group. His loyalty to these concepts was put to the test when one of the men under his charge ran up a huge debt in a gambling den run by a rival gang. Underworld honour demanded that the sinner be killed but, to atone,

Yamamoto resorted to one of the yakuza's traditional diplomatic weapons – cutting off the tip of his own little finger and sending it to the rival gang boss. For good measure, he also cut off the tip of his other little finger at the same time and delivered that to his own boss to assuage his anger. With remarkable understatement, Yamamoto said this self-inflicted damage was a simple thing to do. Yes, there was a lot of pain and dizziness, but he regarded this as routine duty in the service of his superiors.

Although making good his missing finger tips would have helped him to go straight, he steadfastly refused to have one of the operations we had witnessed up north. He said he would defiantly remain a yakuza to the end of his days and people must accept him for what he is. He was also not ashamed to flaunt his full body tattoo, another common badge of honour of the Japanese gangster. His tattoo was based on the story of a young child who conquers a pack of wolves, a vintage yakuza theme of triumphing over great odds.

Backed by a baseball-playing chum from his youth, Yamamoto was trying to develop some skills as a landscape artist. He painted innocent scenes from what he considered to be his idyllic childhood in Japan immediately after the war. There were plenty of happy pastoral family scenes from his rural home village, and nothing of the neon-littered stark cityscapes of Osaka where he plied his trade as a hoodlum.

For him, the decline of the yakuza went hand-in-hand with what he perceived to be the decline of Japan. He believed that the Japanese people had lost their courage;

he said they used to produce fearless kamikaze pilots, but he now felt they would run away from the field of battle – a prospect which frightened him in the current world situation. According to Yamamoto, the Japanese spirit was in great danger of disappearing in a volcano of selfishness.

He knew Japanese society was changing. The antics of the yakuza were no longer tolerated. Because of the gangsters' growing influence, partly achieved through legitimate business dealings during the bubble economy boom of the late eighties, new laws cracking down on their activities had won widespread support. Some human rights lawyers in turn challenged these laws, not out of support for the activities of the mob but because they warned that the government could use them in an authoritarian manner to crack down on other areas of society. Yamamoto, though, appeared to be tolerated by the people as a relic of what was still regarded as the ordered, imperial past. He had abandoned his life of crime but also remained a defiant symbol of attitudes that the modern, business-oriented establishment of Japan was trying to shake off.

While listening to his homespun philosophy, I had a vision of him as a misguided samurai, striding along the old highways of the Shogunate. Like the samurai, Yamamoto gave full obedience to his masters and was prepared to use violence without questioning. Like the samurai, he lived by a rigorous code of honour and, like the samurai, his breed of old-style yakuza has become defunct in modern Japan.

Back in Tokyo, working with Gordon Brewer was a delight, though I did make the fateful mistake of going out drinking with him when he was in a morose mood. It happened inexplicably on the eve of our first day of filming. We ended up at a Mexican restaurant, of all places, eating chicken fajitas and drinking modest amounts of local beer. Then the fun started as I rashly suggested that we try the margaritas on the menu – that was our undoing. For some reason, we ended up ordering ten each. Gordon duly downed all of his. After consuming eight, I was starting to sway alarmingly and had to call it a day. We had got carried away in our eclectic conversations about the psyche of foreign correspondents, death of parents, the fortunes of Glasgow Rangers football club, whether there was a God and, if so, why was the world in such a mess.

I have heard of having bonding sessions before working together, but this was ridiculous. We eventually left the restaurant at 5am when a polite though bemused barman broke the news about the cost of our binge, 35,000 yen – around 125 pounds each. And no, we didn't put it on expenses. They say that a Scotsman never really trusts you until he's got drunk with you, but there must have been a better and cheaper way of establishing a rapport before going filming. Gordon and I had never behaved so irresponsibly just before a shoot or never have done since.

Worse was to follow. I had time for only one and a half hours sleep before I was due to meet the camera crew. Sadly, the alarm clock at the President Hotel in the Aoyama district of Tokyo failed to wake me and I woke up just after the time fixed for our rendezvous. Still extremely hung over, I managed to leap into action, thrust open the wardrobe expecting to find my jackets and shirts, only to discover... nothing. I thought it must be the after effect of the margaritas, but no. After rubbing my eyes hard, there was still nothing to wear – except yesterday's fajita-stained clothes.

I dashed down to reception trying to find an answer to the mystery of the disappearing clothes, only to be told they had been taken away for dry-cleaning as I had instructed. Talk about a language problem! I realised that I had simply mentioned to reception the day before that I needed more coat hangers and they had somehow interpreted that as a request for laundry service. Goodness knows what would have happened had I asked for my shoes to be cleaned. Just a short time out of the gaze of my two redoubtable Japanese fixers and I had fallen into a classic gaijin trap and messed up.

Still, the show had to go on. I made a dash to the tube in my strange-smelling clothes and managed to arrive at the BBC office only about half an hour late. Sadly, the crew had already disappeared, leaving me a note pinned to the door. The Japanese cameraman, Iwata-san, was ruled by an indomitable samurai spirit and he seemed to have an unshakeable belief that it was virtually a hara-kiri offence to be late for a shoot. The problem was that the filming could not go ahead properly without my presence, as only I knew what we were filming and why, so what to do? The rendezvous was at Kanagawa police station in Yokohama about thirty miles away. I had no idea of how to get there by train and it was rush hour. Going by road would therefore be difficult, but that seemed the better of two evils. There was nothing else for it but to hail a taxi.

I had by this stage picked up only a few Japanese words, such as 'domo', or thanks. However, even these paltry attempts at communication proved next to impossible as the alcohol had dulled most of my senses, apart from having a raging thirst. I managed to commandeer a taxi but could not explain where to go. After several minutes of waving my arms around in a poor imitation of a traffic cop, the taxi driver seemed to get the message.

His face brightened visibly: "Ah so.... you mean Kanagawa bang bang."

"Hai", I said, showing what I thought was my extraordinary ability to say yes in Japanese. I was not so chirpy for the rest of the journey as I tried to deal with my aching head.

In the end, I arrived only about a few minutes behind the crew, as the taxi went faster than the crew van. Nonetheless, I was given a reproachful glance by Iwata-san, whom I had met only briefly before. If he had had a ceremonial sword handy, it is possible that he might have asked me to creep away into a corner and do the decent thing. Fuyuko took my antics in good heart. In some ways, the Japanese are unfazed by people with hangovers and happily make allowances for them. Somehow, I managed to get through the day and get the pictures we needed. I did an interview with the chief of police, though I hoped he didn't have a breathalyser to hand.

Throughout the filming schedule, Iwata-san, like the gangster Yamamoto in a vastly different profession, often displayed his keen sense of bushido – keeping to the rigorous code of the samurai. He hated being late, he behaved as if his life was at stake when asked to try something new, and he refused to allow me to carry any of his heavy camera equipment unless I stood my ground and argued for several minutes.

On the infamous hangover-ridden first day of shooting, he was dissatisfied with his filming of a children's kendo class given by a policeman from the Kanagawa Prefecture area. Iwata-san's expression was so sad when he watched the pictures back that I again hoped that no sword was nearby. He insisted on reshooting the whole sequence and ordered his assistant to fix up another kendo class just for the filming. Although I argued that this was not necessary and even said flatly that I would not use it in the final edit, he would have none of it. His honour was at stake and so it was done. In the end, this second attempt at filming did go much better and I even ended up using several shots from the reshoot. Who says the samurai spirit is an outmoded attitude?

Although Iwata-san's devotion to duty was admirable and extremely useful, I was distressed when I saw how the Japanese way of discipline and order could be misused by others. One of the saddest aspects of my stay in Japan was meeting Chisako Tezuka, a delicate Buddhist devotee in her late thirties. I was put in touch with her by a doughty and feisty lawyer called Futaba Igarashi, who had spent her life fighting what she saw as injustices in the legal system and campaigning for human rights. We had asked Futaba to help us find someone who had suffered at the hands of the police when being detained at a police station on suspicion of having committed a crime. At that time, someone could be held at a police station in Japan for up to 23 days without being charged. It was hard to gain access to a lawyer and ill-treatment was rife. The Japanese hold great store by 'washing away one's sin', and confessing to a crime is seen as a way of purging oneself and making it possible to be reintegrated into society. They put more stress on abandoning one's disobedience towards the group than on being punished for the offence. Spending time in a police cell was therefore seen as providing the opportunity to confess. The police rose to their task with zeal, seeing themselves as agents of society in redeeming the errant sinner.

Chisako Tezuka was arrested for allegedly refusing to pay back a loan she had taken out from a friend to help build a hostel for the mentally ill. The police sought to make her confess in a police cell, which is known as a substitute prison. She was held for twenty days, which proved to be a living hell for her. She was strip-searched twice, terrified that a male officer would enter the room while it was taking place. She was humiliated when female officers searched her vagina and anus with their fingers. They also mapped the position of all the moles on her body and meticulously measured her appendix scar. During these examinations and afterwards, she was shouted at, threatened and was the subject of sexual insults. As she remembered these degradations, she sobbed quietly.

The toilet in her police cell had no door and she could be seen from officers passing down a corridor. She had to ask permission before flushing the toilet and spent several hours a day being interrogated while being tethered like a donkey by a rope to a chair. Despite this enormous pressure and humiliation, Chisako refused to confess. She was, after all, completely innocent. She believed she was arrested because of opposition to her building a centre for people who were mentally ill. In Japan, a large number of householders – like many in the UK – do not want such people living near them. Those with such illnesses are an embarrassment, best ignored and kept out of the way. It is easier to pretend they do not exist.

Chisako's stubborn resistance was unusual. Many Japanese in the same position confessed even if they were innocent, partly out of an ingrained deference to authority and partly out of a pragmatic view that they would be treated more leniently if they conformed and subjugated their individual rights to those of society. The legal authorities in turn were uncomfortable with any resistance and it was little wonder that they only allowed defendants to appear in court once they had already become compliant. The overwhelming number of cases that came to court in Japan ended with a guilty verdict, especially as most of the defendants confessed openly to having committing a crime. The authorities did not want any nasty surprises.

Chisako was made to pay heavily for her independent stance. She was adjudged by her family and friends to be a dangerous rebel and so was ostracised by them. When she was released and went home for support after her agonising experience in the police cell, she found her parents had bolted the front door. Her neighbours no longer greeted her, and now they treated her coldly. She felt she could not even walk round her home town. Like virtually everyone else, the newspapers also assumed she must have been guilty because she had been arrested. They continued to hound her for several weeks. It was, after all, a great story for the media. Here was an attractive female Buddhist meditation teacher, apparently being caught with her hands in the till, and compounding her misdemeanours by displaying an unacceptable rebellious streak.

Chisako's was a disturbing tale and I listened to her story with great anger. She was a brave, dignified woman, and it was hard for me to maintain a professional detachment when she broke down in tears when recounting how her calling as a Buddhist teacher had been totally ruined.

Later during our filming period, to preserve good old BBC balance, we carried out a series of interviews with functionaries from the national police agency and the Justice Ministry. They defended the strip searching of prisoners as being necessary to ensure they would be protected from themselves. They also stressed that the whole system of policing, the courts and prisons was based on repentance and keeping harmonious order for the benefit of society as a whole. It was to be my first exposure to how different Asian values are to those of the West, with their emphasis on individual and personal rights and freedoms.

Despite being shocked by the issue of detentions in police cells, we found that our day-to-day contacts with the police were excellent. The individual officers we filmed at a local police sub-station, or Koban, were courteous and helpful. We chose to film at the Kabukicho Koban in the red-light district of Tokyo, in the new, prosperous area of

Shinjuku. It was a weird area of endlessly flashing neon lights, accompanied by a cacophony of raucous music and siren voices urging passers-by to come and partake of the dubious pleasures on offer. Nothing too overt, of course; that is not the Japanese way. Behind the glittering facades lurked a series of sleazy bars, strip-joints and brothels.

On patrol with the police in the Shinjuku area of Tokyo

However, even in such a grubby area, the actual crime rate was very low. The police spent more time helping people who were lost than in being called upon to protect the public from villains. The atmosphere was generally unthreatening and it was a rare sensation to feel completely safe in such a seedy part of a big city. Even at midnight, respectable women could walk along the streets, with the only danger being accosted by a drunken stranger. Here, again, this was not too worrying a prospect. For some reason, most Japanese appeared to be completely harmless and passive when intoxicated. Instead of producing aggression, a surfeit of alcohol led to an appealing helplessness. The revellers acted more like a tipsy Stan Laurel would have done – innocent smiles and engaging displays of trust and affectionate friendship.

We also felt safe in other parts of the city, despite displays of lawlessness. Late one Saturday night, we caught up with a couple of hundred young people who were setting up an illegal racing track on a public road on the outskirts of Yokohama. Sleek cars with powerful engines lined up two-by-two in front of a skinny youth who acted as starter for the race. Although this event was an act of rebellion, there was no real menace in the air and this was relatively mild hooliganism. In fact, the hot-rodders showed their true colours when just a single police car showed up and, via a loudspeaker, ordered everyone to go home. There were no protests or histrionics; everyone complied and meekly slinked away. It was if there was an unspoken contract that people could let off steam up to a point, but everyone knew where the line was and few were willing to cross it.

Eating was a welcome distraction to trying to understand the intricate Japanese attitudes to law and order, confession, and authority. I blanched at raw squid leg and most other morsels served up under the collective name of sashimi, but I did enjoy the head of tuna (maguro), pork, and other meats fried in batter (tempura). There was only one sticky moment when I was taken out by a lawyer who had acted for the yakuza in Osaka. He took us to a traditional restaurant where you knelt at the table and sampled a myriad of local delicacies. One turned out to be an expensive dish of puffer fish called fugu, parts of which are deadly poisonous. What was I to do? Offend my host by refusing to eat it and jeopardise the chance of gaining inside information or throw caution to the wind and run the risk of being poisoned for the good old Beeb? In the end, reckless curiosity got the better of me and so I reached out falteringly with my chopsticks, grabbed a piece of innocuous-looking white flesh and chewed. It didn't taste of much. It wasn't worth the huge price and certainly not worth the risk of death. Chefs are specially trained of course not to serve up the toxic parts of the fugu but there is the occasional mistake, which fortunately did not occur that night in Osaka.

Overall, Japan was a fascinating amalgam of experiences. I admired the politeness and sense of order and the friendship that was shown to me, but I did feel uneasy at the seemingly unquestioning loyalty of many of its people and the prejudice that lay just beneath the surface. The bureaucracy in Japan had huge power and control, and seemed answerable to no-one, least of all the country's corrupt politicians and biddable population.

My attitude to the Japanese state apparatus became even worse when I had a postcard a few months later after my law and order film was broadcast. It was from a friend of the Buddhist meditation teacher, Chisako. The friend had watched the film on *BBC World*. She had noted my name in the credits and wrote saying that she had some bad news for me; she said that Chisako could no longer bear the increasing strain she had been under because of her refusal to conform and had committed suicide. It was a tragic footnote to my first visit to the Land of the Rising Sun.

A few months later, I was back in Japan again, this time to make a film about the growing pressure from nationalist right-wing groups for the country to use its new economic prowess to assert itself on the world stage. Such groups were pressing for Japan to seek a permanent seat on the United Nations Security Council and to contest the post-war settlement that Japan was not allowed to have regular armed forces. This was another controversial and disturbing topic to pursue.

During the visit, we interviewed Shintaro Ishihara, who had co-authored a hard-hitting book in the late eighties called *The Japan That Can Say No*. This book urged the Japanese to contest American dominance and take a much more independent line in international and business affairs. Ishihara went on to become Governor of Tokyo in 1999 and continued to make controversial statements about other countries and even his own. He had to apologise after claiming that the Japanese earthquake and tsunami of 2011 was a divine punishment because the Japanese people had become too materially and financially greedy.

Under the constitution written by the United States after the Second World War, Japan was not allowed to maintain any armed forces with an offensive capability. However, it was allowed to establish a self-defence force to help maintain security within the country itself. We saw for ourselves how these forces operated when we filmed some manoeuvres at the Natashino military ground in Tokyo, where, around a century previously, the Meiji emperor had reviewed imperial forces.

It was a time of change for the self-defence forces, as Japan had recently sent troops to join the Cambodia peace-keeping mission – the first time any Japanese soldiers had been allowed to go on a mission on foreign soil since the end of the war. But the continuing American military presence was also very obvious in Japan. We filmed a US military unit on manoeuvres based in the shadow of Mount Fuji, just a small cog among the thousands of American troops stationed in Japan after 1945. From our briefings, it was abundantly clear that the Americans would not be leaving any time soon.

On a research trip to the site of the Hiroshima nuclear bomb

While making the documentary, we also travelled to Hawaii and went to Pearl Harbour, scene of the Japanese attack in 1941 which dramatically changed the course of World War Two. We filmed the wreck of the USS Arizona, which was sunk with the loss of more than a thousand lives. It was possible to see the number 3 gun turret sticking up, with a small leak of oil still coming to surface after more than half a century. The consequences of the Pearl Harbour strike continue to reverberate around the Pacific and East Asia to this day.

CHAPTER TWELVE

The Balkans Kaleidoscope

The break-up of Yugoslavia in the early nineties created one of the biggest convulsions in recent history. It led to a number of vicious wars and the emergence of a new, chilling vocabulary: ethnic cleansing. This phrase described how some communities were systemically and ruthlessly hunted down, and either killed or moved to other areas. Even to this day, around twenty years on, there are still international troops stationed in two of the countries which emerged from the break-up, Bosnia and Kosovo. Over the last decade or so, I have visited the Balkans on numerous occasions. I have spent some time in Croatia and Serbia and stayed for long periods helping to transform state broadcasting organisations in both Montenegro and Bosnia.

However, it is Kosovo I know best and have witnessed over the years how it has emerged from the end of the war there to declaring itself an independent state in 2008. I have worked with many students on a Masters' programme in journalism and have been amazed and sometimes shocked by the ideas they have come up with for their documentary projects. This is the part of the world which has suffered searing hatred and pain.

One student, Bardh, made a film about Mrs Cerkezi, a woman from the town of Gjakova who lost her husband and four sons during the war. Nearly a decade later, she still had no news of any of them and had no idea where their bodies were. She was even still harbouring hopes that one or more of them would suddenly turn up back home alive. It was a tough documentary to watch. Mrs Cerkezi's house had now become a kind of living museum, with photos and clothes of her missing family on display. Altogether more than 800 people were declared missing or killed in Gjakova because of the war. The grief caused still weighed down heavily on several people I met from the area.

On a brighter note, it has been a joy to see the optimism engendered by the independence declaration. However, the new country obviously still has a long way to go to rid itself of the scars from the war and become prosperous and stable. Tension also remains between Serbs and Kosovar Albanians in some parts of Kosovo, including the northern divided town of Mitrovica. I first visited the town in the autumn of 2000, less than 18 months after the end of the Kosovo War. My diary of that trip and a subsequent visit shortly afterwards follows below.

MITROVICA DIARY

SUNDAY 22 OCTOBER

My first view of Kosovo from the air is dramatic – a vast green plain sandwiched between big mountains. The airfield is tiny but there are also many military helicopters hidden under camouflage netting. As the plane is taxiing in, it nearly runs over a dog. When I leave the airport, there is no-one to meet me, despite a promise I would be looked after by the organisation I am working for, the Organisation for Security and Co-operation in Europe, or OSCE for short.

After a worrying few minutes, a Kosovar Albanian turns up with a scruffy sign bearing my name. He drives me straight to Mitrovica in his white Toyota jeep, one of many hundred such vehicles being used by the international community in Kosovo. By the roadside, houses are being rebuilt everywhere, with their red brick walls and red roofs glistening in the sunlight. It is a shock to see the scale of the destruction caused by the Serbian attacks and this is now 18 months after the conflict ended. The driver gives me a running commentary in faltering English.

"Maybe in ten years it will all be OK," he says. He is perplexed that I do not have an official call sign when he is in radio contact with base giving our movements.

On the way, we skirt past the capital, Pristina, and I see the Kosovo Polje monument, a hated symbol of Serbian nationalism in Kosovo. The monument commemorates the battle here in 1389 when Serbian forces headed by Prince Lazar were defeated by the Turks. Now the site is fenced off and heavily guarded by KFOR troops to prevent attacks by Albanian extremists.

We have to take a detour round a bridge destroyed by NATO when it was trying to drive out the Serbian army. Eventually, we enter Mitrovica and reach the OSCE compound. I meet the organisation's press officer, a cheerful German called Hanns-Christian Klasing. He takes me on a tour across the main bridge over the River Ibar, with its barbed wire and posse of French troops on guard. Hanns points out three heavily-protected blocks of Albanian flats on the Serbian side north of the river. I am really shocked by the destruction of what used to be the Roma area on the Albanian side. This was carried out as a reprisal just after the war, as the Roma were seen by Albanians as Serbian collaborators.

We drive past the huge Trepča smelting complex, a relic from the days of Yugoslavia. I am going to be working with Serbian journalists in their part of town, so we also visit three Serbian radio stations, one based in a tiny living room and two others in the centre of the town. One station, Contact Plus, has quite good equipment and replays some BBC output during parts of the day. The Motel Biševac, my base for the next ten days, is a surprisingly attractive building amid all the dowdy-looking blocks of flats, no doubt built by communism's finest architects!

In the back of the building, I meet my translator, Ivan. As we talk about the upcoming training course, about eight French soldiers in full uniform come in and sit down for a meal. Ivan also briefs me about the mysterious death of one French soldier in the Albanian flats area and warns me about the bridge-watchers. They are Serbian hard-liners who stand guard unofficially at the main bridge and constantly cause trouble.

My room is basic but comfortable enough. One snag though is that the water goes off every day between 10pm and 6am. The pipes gurgling into life after a night of inactivity act as a bizarre sort of alarm clock.

MONDAY 23 OCTOBER

My course for Serbian radio journalists starts late. I am not sure whether this is due to Serbian time-keeping or logistical problems. I quickly send the students out of a classroom setting to gather stories. They come back with ideas ranging from a kindergarten strike to petrol shortages to banking problems. The students also find a happy tale about a prostitute; now she has found true love and given up her trade. One local station is playing a happy love song dedicated to her.

We ask for a light lunch at the Biševac but we are provided with large portions of pork, potatoes and tasty, warm bread. Pork is a speciality here, apparently. Every day a whole pig is roasted outside on a special barbecue. Ivan takes me along the main street, where there are many makeshift little kiosks selling bottled drinks and chocolates in a desperate effort to survive. We go over to Ivan's flat where he is staying with his girlfriend, who works as a translator at a radio station for French forces. He tells me that phone calls are free, even international ones. No-one is collecting the bills, though the network is somehow functioning.

TUESDAY 24 OCTOBER

I have an early morning walk around town. I first go to an area near the river which is heavily patrolled, as there are houses belonging to Albanians, Turks, and Bosniaks (Slavs who have converted to Islam). Numbers on the course are down, mainly due to a security alert further north.

After today's session I go for another stroll, this time across the main bridge into the Albanian part of town.

This area is much more populated, with more of a Middle Eastern feel. I am surprised at how many restaurants are open and at the number of well-stocked shops with fruit and vegetables. On the down side, there are many damaged houses and piles of rubbish everywhere. After I emerge from the bridge on to the Serbian side, I am accosted by two bridge-watchers. They curtly ask me who I am but seem content after I produce my trusty BBC identity card.

WEDNESDAY 25 OCTOBER

Everything is thrown up in the air on the course as we hear that an important press conference is to be given by Richard Holbrooke, US Ambassador to the UN and former special envoy to the Balkans. It was Holbrooke who chillingly told the Serbian leader Slobodan Milošević to his face in 1999 that his country would be bombed unless he agreed to pull out his forces from Kosovo. All my students are keen to attend the press conference and see what Holbrooke has to say, but they are also a little frightened because the event is to be held in the optimistically named 'confidence zone', a secure neutral area on the Albanian side.

Eventually, the students pluck up their courage and agree to walk across the bridge. The press conference turns out to be a shambles. Holbrooke begins his statement before all the five television crews are ready and while dozens of newspaper journalists are still coming into the room. Lots of pushing and shoving ensues. Most of the students do not have a clue what is going on, as the promised translation into Serbian does not materialise.

Back at the hotel late at night, the owner invites me to have some slivovitz, or plum brandy. I politely accept, but decline a second as my insides are still burning after the first glass.

The bridge between the two divided parts of Mitrovica

FRIDAY 27 OCTOBER

I wake early as I am full of Slovenian and Serbian beer from last night. I feel ill all morning. It is hard not to become fed up with the huge quantities of meat constantly on offer, all with fat everywhere. Even my eggs this morning are swimming in it.

The course goes well as we receive a surprise visit from Zorka, a BBC stringer whom I met at the Holbrooke press conference. She inspires the students by stressing how important it is to have a love of the job you are doing. I feel sick over lunch but later sit out on a bench in the sun, have a doze and then recover. In the evening, strong winds and rain suddenly arrive – winter is coming.

SATURDAY 28 OCTOBER

Today we go to another press conference linked to the results of local elections in Kosovo. This time it is in an OSCE building outside the confidence area. Hanns has to come and meet the students and ferry them by car in relays to the meeting. I walk over the bridge. The mood of the conference is upbeat, but my Serbian students are not impressed, as their community is boycotting the elections. It is something of a farce when voting figures are given for Serbian areas. There are no voters at all in Leposavić and just one in Zvečan.

Ivan tells me after the press conference that four of my students were terrified after Hanns had to leave them alone at the OSCE building with just a couple of Albanian guards. Things can so easily get out of control here. Later, I go back to a second news conference with Tanya. She earlier had her tape confiscated by the bridge-watchers when she went to record material at a voting station in the Bosniak area.

Afterwards, Hanns is invited to coffee with three Albanian women. I join them and so eventually does Tanya. It is tense at first but after a while all is well. These are the first attempts at reconciliation but obviously it will all take a long time. Later, I go back to the south and am in gastronomic heaven as I buy a tuna sandwich, a change from all the hard-core meat I am continually being fed in the Serbian quarter. The area is in darkness due to a power failure and the noise of the large generators is a bit spooky.

SUNDAY 29 OCTOBER

I am awake early again after finding it difficult to sleep. I ask for scrambled eggs in Serbian – kajgana – and am pathetically proud that I can now speak around 30 words of the language. I give the students a tough assignment involving making a radio feature.

In the afternoon, I ring home from Ivan's flat. The call is free, of course. My 12-year-old son Tim tells me that he and his older brother Phil have been playing football in the garden and have muddied the lawn. I try to muster my best indignant fatherly response but my heart is not in it. A wrecked lawn just does not seem important compared to the problems here in Mitrovica, where people are living in cellars and Mafia thugs are crawling all around.

I make a mistake when out at a restaurant with Hanns on the south side of the town. I toast him using the Serbian word, zhiveli, but luckily no Albanian is within earshot to take offence. That will teach me to be so bushy-tailed about my self-imagined prowess in Serbian.

MONDAY 30 OCTOBER

It is a cold and frosty start to the day. I am still not sleeping properly. Maybe it is due to the noisy KFOR (Kosovo Force) tanks which rumble on patrol throughout the night. Or maybe it is over-stimulation of the brain or repressed anxiety. One simple explanation could be that any insomnia is simply due to the steak and chips, and red Macedonian wine I had for dinner last night.

Hanns arranges a meeting with Oliver Ivanović, the leader of the Serbs in Mitrovica. I do not like his cold eyes. He is a former karate teacher and is deeply distrusted by the Kosovar Albanians. He is very dismissive of any chances of reconciliation between the two communities.

We also hear that two French soldiers have been beaten after a sweep for weapons in a Serbian enclave goes wrong. In the evening several students from the course come out for a farewell drink. There are a surprising amount of bars open but no-one is in a mood to celebrate.

TUESDAY 31 OCTOBER

The students replay their radio features at the end of the course. It has been a very rewarding experience for us all. We have some more pork for lunch and then I am taken by jeep to Pristina. It is a scary journey, with tanks, jeeps and tractors and private cars all jostling for position on a narrow road.

Bomb damage caused to the former Serb police headquarters in Pristina

Pristina is much bigger than I thought it would be. I see the former police station, which was flattened by a NATO bomb. There is little military activity here but there are hundreds of UN/OSCE jeeps. I am staying in the gigantic Grand Hotel, a bit of a communist relic. It was here where the notorious Serbian paramilitary leader, Arkan, tortured some Kosovar Albanians.

* * *

I returned to Kosovo around three months later to complete the radio training in Mitrovica.

* * *

SATURDAY 10 FEBRUARY 2001

On my second visit to Kosovo, I am met by an OSCE driver and Elizabeta, who is helping to organise the second part of the journalist training. She tells me that Pristina is fairly quiet, though its population is continuing to expand as Albanians from the rest of Kosovo flock in to seek work and shelter. Elizabeta is in despair at a recent outbreak of tension and violence in Mitrovica, when a number of French KFOR troops were attacked by angry Albanians who accused them of siding with the Serbs.

The traffic in Pristina is chaotic.

"Just like Manhattan," grumbles my driver.

Certainly it is hard to move amid the incredible number of UN, OSCE and police jeeps which career around the untidy and dusty streets. After picking up my KFOR press accreditation, I check in at the huge Grand Hotel. It is trying to shake off its run-down communist image and has smart new lifts and new carpets in the rooms.

While going for a stroll later, the problems of this city are all too apparent. Many small restaurants are lit by candles due to the latest power cut. Noisy juddering generators provide electricity for some of the bigger properties, but at the cost of many people's ear-drums.

SUNDAY 11 FEBRUARY

I leave the Grand Hotel at 10am and am picked up by an OSCE driver to go on the depressing road north to Mitrovica. The town is instantly recognisable from a distance because of its huge red and white chimney belonging to the giant Trepča smelting works. Approaching from the south, we come across the Serbian church, the only place in the Albanian part of town where any Serbs live. Here, about twenty church workers and their families manage some kind of existence protected by KFOR tanks. They are effectively hostages, though perhaps their real protection comes from the fact there are about 3,000 Albanians in a similar situation living in isolated pockets among the 15,000 strong Serbian community in the north of the town.

I am met at the OSCE headquarters by the local press officer, Hanns, who tells me of a recent terrifying ordeal endured by six Serbs working for the OSCE. A few days ago they were stopped by a group of angry Albanians in the south and pulled out of their vehicle. One man was nearly beaten to death and a Serbian woman was abducted in a car by an Albanian but managed to talk her way to freedom. The others were rescued by some Belgian troops but have been so traumatised that they have not yet returned to work in the OSCE HQ in the south.

Over lunch with Hanns and two OSCE colleagues, we talk about the prospects for peace. The recent trouble has put everything into reverse. The plans to set up a joint political process, a multi-ethnic radio station, even the hopes of national elections, are all in jeopardy. The trouble has apparently been stoked by Serbian political factions and Albanian extremists who, after losing ground in the recent municipal elections, are now keen to win the battle for the streets.

Lack of money is not a major problem at the moment. There are huge amounts of cash swilling around – not just from the massive international presence but also from Kosovar Albanians working elsewhere in Europe, who send back cash to help their families still in Kosovo. However, the continuing problems with ethnic violence, human trafficking, drug-running, and weapons smuggling all make for one big mess.

I am staying again at the Motel Biševac, which as usual is populated by listless men in black leather jackets, who gather to smoke and drink the viciously strong coffee with no milk. And yes, pork is on the menu yet again. The electricity is off and no doubt the water will go off during the night as well.

MONDAY 12 FEBRUARY

I am right about the water; the pipes rattled and shook at around 10pm last night to mark the death throes of the supply. The water comes back on to the sound of clanking pipes at around 6.30am. I am reminded that you do not need an early morning call at the Motel Biševac.

It has been a somewhat disturbed night. I didn't hear any NATO vehicles on patrol this time but, incredibly, someone seems to have been using a vacuum cleaner for ages from around midnight. As they say, you don't have to be mad to stay in northern Mitrovica, but it certainly helps.

I am determined to start the course promptly at 9am, but I suppose I should have known better. Many of the participants work at some of the tiny radio stations scattered around the Serbian areas. We are also joined by a Serbian employee of the OSCE, who was one of those attacked in the south a few days ago. She is still shaken and declares wistfully that she does not think she will be returning again to the south.

"At least I am still alive," she smiles ruefully.

We eventually get cracking about 20 minutes late and I outline the aims of the course – to produce our own news bulletin by Thursday. It is hard here to foster a notion of a free, independent and vigorous press. First, there were 40 or so years of communism, and then more than a decade of rampant nationalism under Milošević. It is difficult to question authority and often it is far safer to say nothing, even when you know things to be wrong.

One of the men from Leposavić gives us a graphic example of intimidation. Just before Christmas, an extremist Serb was arrested in the town for drunken driving. His hot-head friends believed this was a political injustice and wanted to mobilise the Serbian population to protest against the authorities. Some extremists went to the three radio stations in the area and demanded that they all broadcast an appeal for people to come out onto the streets. In the resulting demonstration, two people died after Belgian troops fired shots to try to keep the crowd under control. It meant that abuse of the media directly led to death – a salutary tale.

In the evening, I head briefly for the Albanian south side to escape yet another dose of pork. The area round the bridge is quiet at the moment but, as everyone keeps warning me, it only takes a spark for violence to flare up again.

Late in the evening, I go for a coffee with my translator, Ivan, who fills me in on how the twenty-somethings of Serbia have been blighted by a decade of Milošević's leadership. Many are now unemployed due to economic mismanagement and international sanctions during the Milošević era. The resulting lack of purpose and money has meant that young people find it hard to socialise and it is difficult to meet a prospective marriage partner. The cost of bringing up a family is also a daunting prospect in a country where the average wage is still around 100 DMs a month – just over 30 pounds.

So if you are a Serbian young man and fancy a particular girl, it is hard to ask her out because there are very few suitable places to go to such as cinemas and discos. It is also embarrassing not to be able to afford to buy her a drink or meal, and degrading to admit that you are jobless and have no prospects. As a result, both sexes find themselves trapped in a cycle of despair, often living at home with their parents and unable to envisage how they can get a job, let alone a satisfying career and family.

Of course, it is different in the sophisticated surroundings of Belgrade but you have to have contacts there to survive. The plum jobs depend greatly on what Ivan calls the magic circle – the nexus of family and close friends who protect their own and allow very few others to break in.

Back at the hotel, the phantom vacuum cleaner is at it again between midnight and 1pm. It turns out that because of the low voltage of the electricity supply during the day, the only time that vacuum cleaners can work effectively is when there is much less demand on the system late at night.

TUESDAY 13 FEBRUARY

The day dawns much colder, but there is still no sign of the freezing conditions I am expecting. We go to another OSCE press conference, which I film with my own hi-8 camera. Interestingly, this is now one of the few environments in which Albanians and Serbians can be in the same room without violence. Thankfully, the common cause of journalism seems to transcend at least the worst of bitter ethnic hatreds.

It is clear though that the political process is in a mess, with KFOR and the UN right in the middle between the two communities. One sticking point is an Albanian wish, backed by the international community, to extend the confidence area to the north of the bridge. This is, of course, seen by the Serbs as a big provocation and an attack on their land.

At the end of the day I wander again across the bridge to the south. Groups of French mountain troops with their floppy black berets are huddled round a burning brassier. So are the bridge-watchers on the Serbian side. In the south there is yet another power cut. It is all depressingly part of the routine here.

WEDNESDAY 14 FEBRUARY

The practical problems of operating in a place like Mitrovica hit home this morning; two groups of students from Leposavić and a nearby enclave called Zubin Potok are delayed due to security problems. Yesterday at least three Serbs were injured in that region when their tractor ran over a landmine, presumably planted by Albanians. So the course starts one hour late. After the opening pleasantries of cigarettes and strong dark coffee, it is down to work.

Instead of pork, there is lamb for lunch today. Hooray! Over the meal, I chat to two guys from Zubin Potok. They lead very difficult and dangerous lives. Sometimes the only way they can get to Mitrovica is by foot – a lonely walk of four hours across hazardous territory. One of them freely admits that it is impossible to broadcast news at the moment in such a charged environment. Sticking to music is the only safe option.

All of the students are depressed by the moves to create a new secure confidence zone north of the river. They see it merely as a way of resettling more Albanians in the north and ultimately driving the Serbs out of Kosovo altogether. Where, they say, are the attempts to resettle any Serbs back in their former homes in the south?

After lunch, the students go out to collect some stories, including one at the prison where two Serbs accused of raping some Albanian women are on hunger strike.

In the evening I go for a pizza by myself to escape the Biševac and climb the hill to reach the nicest part of town, though it is all relative. Here there are some spacious villas with pleasant gardens. Even in this area, the long shadow of violence intrudes as the occasional house stands burnt out. They are clearly the former homes of Albanians who, at one time, lived happily together with Serbs.

THURSDAY 15 FEBRUARY

Today we face the moment of truth: will we manage to get our own planned news bulletin on air? Two of the students go to cover another OSCE press conference and are annoyed because they have to wait for transport back from the south side of the bridge in the confidence area. While standing there in a vulnerable position, they are taunted by some angry Albanians – a very unpleasant incident, given the problems of recent weeks. There are also reports that a Serb who works for an international agency has gone missing in the unstable region of Preševo while on assignment. Danger and violence surrounds you all the time here.

In the afternoon the Biševac conference room is beginning to hum like a typical newsroom. It is very satisfying. At one stage, we are running late with scripts and have problems completing the edits of the packages. The final straw comes when the power goes out as we are printing the running order. It is time for a good belly laugh – what else can you do?

In the end, we make it to the Contact Plus station and, after yet more hassles and misunderstandings, manage to record an 11-minute bulletin. The sound proofing is not brilliant and, of course, at key moments a KFOR tank rattles along the road outside. But overall the students manage very well. They depart totally exhausted, bewildered by the speed of thought needed to put out a live news bulletin. It's a good buzz to see some of them, as one student put it, falling in love with journalism.

FRIDAY 16 FEBRUARY

It is the final day of the course. I am relieved to be going home. The phantom vacuum cleaner was at it again at midnight and the huge bulky pillow on my bed is definitely taking its toll on my neck muscles. I am hoping the course will have a gentle wind-down, but again the unpredictability of journalism strikes. We are told that the overall KFOR head, General Carlo Cabigiosu, is giving a press conference at the hospital in the northern part of Mitrovica at 10am, so I take all the students along for a first-hand seat.

The press conference itself is chaotic, with many French soldiers present in a show of force. There are quite a lot of Serbian journalists and a few Albanians, who have shown considerable bravery in venturing into the north. The General is guarded by a particularly frightening soldier with a flinty glare and menacing machine gun at the ready.

The main issue is whether the prominent Serbian politician, Oliver Ivanović, is going to be part of the official talks over the future of Mitrovica. After the press conference, much to everyone's surprise, a couple of hundred demonstrators gather outside chanting anti-KFOR slogans. Many of them are hospital staff, dressed in their white coats and carrying placards denouncing the general. The anti-NATO resentment has been fuelled by worries over the proposed confidence zone extension. The general drives off in convoy, protected by tanks and other armoured vehicles.

Back at the Biševac, there are more surprises, confirming how unpredictable and unstable a region this is. We receive a call saying that a number of Serbs have been killed by a mine as they were travelling in a bus in a KFOR convoy in eastern Kosovo. Everyone is shocked, angry and frightened. Hanns calls me to say that I should end the course as soon as possible because the OSCE is restricting freedom of movement in case there is hostile reaction to the bombing. He comes over to fetch me in an armoured jeep. As we pass the north side of the bridge, dozens of bridge-watchers are gathering in an agitated and intimidating manner.

Once over the bridge, we hear that there have also been reports of another attack on a Serb bus in southern Kosovo, but these turn out to be false. We travel in an armoured Cherokee jeep, which is very cramped inside. I hate the journey along the road to Pristina; several military vehicles in convoy slow everyone down and the small, lethargic tractors are a constant hazard. The prospect of being injured in civilian disturbances is real, though probably remote, but the danger of being injured or killed in the chaotic driving conditions is much more likely. While I am thinking these morbid thoughts, a stray dog dashes out in front of us and the heavy jeep runs over it with a sickening thud.

For the rest of the trip, I am on edge, especially when children walk ominously close to the side of the road in gathering darkness. I cannot erase the image of the mangled corpse of the dog lying in the road and fervently hope a child will not rush out and go under our wheels.

After quickly checking into the Grand in Pristina, I make my way to the modern high-rise OSCE building. On the top floor Happy Hour is just getting underway at the bar. All drinks cost just 50p and there is lively disco music blaring out. Everything should be in place for a relaxing time but the atmosphere is totally gloomy. The Serbs killed and injured in the bus convoy were on their way back to the settlement of Gračanica, a Serb enclave just south of Pristina. Several Serbs from there work at the OSCE building in Pristina, and their shock and grief have quickly spread around the building.

The internationals I talk to amid the strains of Abba are all distraught. Much of what they have been working for has now been dealt a severe blow. As we chat, a TV screen in the bar displays pictures of the Serbian bus destroyed in the landmine explosion. It is totally wrecked – a wire bomb planted under the noses of the KFOR protecting convoy. This is a frightening escalation in the conflict here. The obvious suspects are extremist Albanians frustrated by the diminishing prospects for independence. They are now trying to drive the remaining Serbs out of Kosovo by deliberate organised terror tactics. We consume our drinks quickly – a classic case of trying to drown your sorrows.

One OSCE worker tells me the horrifying story of a Bulgarian worker a few months ago who had come to work for the organisation in Pristina. On his first night in town, an Albanian spoke to him in Serbian as a ruse. Because the worker understood the language, he replied in Serbian and was promptly shot dead on the spot. It is a sobering tale and I remind myself to banish the few Serbian words I have picked up from my mind. *Think English, think English*, I tell myself.

I leave the bar around 9pm, chew my way through a quick plate of pasta and go to bed. At least there is a decent pillow at this hotel and there is no phantom vacuum-cleaner. Nevertheless, the water goes off all night just to make me feel at home.

SATURDAY 17 FEBRUARY

Again, the day dawns bright and sunny. I need something to lift my spirits, though I know deep down that I am relieved to be going home. While my OSCE driver is taking me to the airport, I ask him what he thinks of the land mine attack yesterday. There is no hesitation. He says that, one hundred per cent, it was the work of Serbs themselves, just to make trouble and damage the Albanian cause. That is how it goes here – never concede an inch to the other side and always assume the worst of them. The constant smell of danger and tension in the air has taken its toll and I am very glad to board the Swiss Air flight to Zurich and civilisation.

CHAPTER THIRTEEN

Transformation in Ethiopia

September 11 is a date etched into our collective conscience but for me this date has also come to mean something else. September 11 is also the start of the New Year in Ethiopia, a country I have grown to love, having made more than forty trips there on various teaching and training assignments over the last decade or so.

The Ethiopian Calendar and calculation of time is different to that in the West. The Ethiopians celebrated their millennium more than seven years after most of the rest of the world and the hour of the day is calculated from dawn, not from midnight. For example, 11am in the West is just five o'clock in the morning in Ethiopia, a difference of six hours which is maintained throughout the day. No wonder there is constant confusion when foreigners, known everywhere in Ethiopia as 'ferengis', try to fix an appointment with locals.

Ethiopia is trying hard to shake off its international image as a drought-ridden, basket case country following the well-publicised famine of 1984. On my first visit there in 2001 (Western calendar!), I immediately became aware of how many Ethiopians are understandably upset about how their country is seen by the rest of the world. They point proudly to Ethiopia's unique history in Africa. They stress that it has never been colonised, and embraced Christianity long before European countries. The spectacular 12th Century rock-hewn churches of Lalibela in the north are rightly celebrated. In many parts of the country, there is plenty of rain and potentially fertile areas waiting to be exploited. Ethiopia is far from being a gigantic dust bowl.

Sharing a joke with students on the compound of Addis Ababa University

The nation is very diverse, with more than 80 languages spoken by ethnic groups across the country. The food is unique and the Ethiopians love their ubiquitous injera, a pancake-like flatbread made of teff grain, used to soak up spicy varieties of wat or stews. The energetic dancing styles are also spectacular, including the iskista, which involves rapid and exuberant shaking of the shoulders.

In the last few years, Ethiopia has also been subjected to tremendous social and economic change. It now has one of the fastest growing economies in the world, with widespread investment in roads, shopping malls and other infrastructure. Each time I go back to Addis, I am amazed to see yet more buildings springing up or another flyover completed. The government is determined to carry out an ambitious five-year growth and transformation plan in a country which already has the second largest population in Africa – at around 90 million people – and is still growing fast.

THE CHINESE IN AFRICA

Spending so much time in Ethiopia has given me the chance to see an example of how the Chinese are working throughout Africa. Many countries on the continent are bewitched by China's attitude to development. Unlike Western governments, the Chinese do not harp on about linking international aid to human rights policy. They simply hand out large sums of cash in return for access to minerals and local markets for Chinese goods. Ten years ago, there was hardly a Chinese face to be seen in Ethiopia; now there are plenty, as Chinese workers pour in to work on building roads, railways, and shopping malls. They are also advising on large-scale manufacturing and agricultural projects.

One of the biggest symbols of the Chinese presence in Africa is the new shiny glass and steel headquarters for the African Union, which is based in Addis Ababa. It was completed on schedule at the start of 2012 at a cost of 200 million US dollars. All the money came from the Chinese government as a no-strings-attached gift, and the building work was carried out by Chinese know-how on the ground. The sleek and towering office block next to a U-shaped, state-of-the-art conference centre has twenty stories. Visitors to the block can reportedly go to a height of 99.9 metres to symbolise the day that the now-defunct Organisation of African Unity voted to form the African Union on 9 September 1999.

On a visit to Addis in January 2012, one of my AU contacts, whose office overlooks the newly completed AU headquarters, expressed a trenchant opinion about it.

"China has shamed Africa," he lamented. He was impressed by Chinese efficiency but depressed by the failure of African states to be able to come together and construct such a building for themselves.

On a filming trip to Malawi for the African Union in 2011, I also saw a huge swanky building going up, which was to serve as the AU's southern headquarters. Yes, you've guessed it: the Chinese funded that one too.

In 2011 the BBC was reporting that the trade between China and Africa was worth 120 billion US dollars. It is clear that this story is far from finished and is one of the biggest drivers of change the African continent has ever seen.

A COUNTRY OF RUNNERS

I am standing in the sun with my 15-year-old son Tim by the side of a race track in the modest, no-frills sports stadium in Addis Ababa. We are waiting to catch a glimpse of one of the greatest long distance runners the world has ever seen, Haile Gebrselassie. By now, he has already won two Olympic golds in the 10,000 metres and four World Championship medals in the same event. Somehow we have managed to worm our way into the stadium to watch a number of Ethiopian athletes go through their training routines ahead of the upcoming 2004 Olympic Games in Athens.

As the minutes tick by, our sense of anticipation grows. Finally, we see Haile in the distance, a very slight figure in a green and yellow track suit, ambling effortlessly towards us to the entrance onto the track. When he reaches us, he gives us a polite grin and says good morning. My son is star struck and, if I am honest, so am I. We mumble a greeting in return and see him go on to the track to start his warm-up routines.

We revel in this opportunity to watch such an elite athlete at work and the minutes pass by quickly. Our contentment is suddenly interrupted when we are summoned to a small office in the back of the main stand. A burly, scary man inside the office is very angry. He demands to know who we are and how we have managed to get into a closed training session. It turns out that he is one of the main coaches in charge and he is in no mood to listen to our attempts to explain our presence.

With a flourish of his arms, Mr Angry accuses us of spying for the Kenyan athletics team, Ethiopia's long-term rivals in long-distance running. I have been suspected of many things in my journalistic career, but this really tops it all. We are ordered out of the stadium forthwith and are left only with our happy memories of having witnessed one of nature's thoroughbreds in action.

Ethiopia's sporting prowess has always been in long-distance running, but in recent times there are signs that this may be about to change. Young Ethiopian runners are now taking an interest in middle distance events such as the 800 metres. Just before the 2012 Olympics, I was the executive producer of a film about Ethiopian emerging stars preparing for the Games. One of the characters chosen was Mohammed Aman, who at 18 had a real chance of winning a medal at the London games.

In the event Mohammed ran a personal best time and broke the Ethiopian national record in the Olympics 800 metres final which was won in world-record time by David Rudisha of Kenya. Despite his strong performance, Mohammed finished only sixth in the race. However, a

Tesfalem Gebru on an early morning training run in his home town of Adigrat in northern Ethiopia.

few weeks later in Zurich he confirmed his considerable promise when he imposed a rare defeat on Rudisha.

Another young person profiled in the film was Yanet Seyoum, the first Ethiopian female swimmer to take part in the Olympics.

Our final character was Tesfalem Gebru, a Paralympic middle distance runner. We visited his house in the town of Adigrat, way up in the north of Ethiopia near the Eritrean border.

As a young boy more than a decade ago, his hand was blown off when his house was bombed by a plane from Eritrea during its war with Ethiopia. His mother, who still lives at the same house, believed her life was over when she saw how badly injured he was, but now is overjoyed

Tesfalem being interviewed at his house damaged in the war between Ethiopia and Eritrea

to see his progress. The damage to the roof of their home has still not been repaired, but Tesfalem gamely posed for photographs in front of the ruins.

In his home town Tesfalem is very popular, and we filmed him holding training sessions at the local stadium for other disabled runners. Some of them are deaf and communicated with each other in sign language. One young girl with a charming smile sat in an improvised wheelchair with a white plastic seat. She found it hard to push her wheelchair on the bumpy track but was nonetheless determined to do her best for our camera. It was encouraging to see that someone like Tesfalem is helping to inspire others and change the attitudes of some Ethiopians towards disability.

On location with our crew filming at the stadium in Adigrat

ON LOCATION WITH THE MURSI

Ever since my first trip to Ethiopia, I have been fascinated and maybe a little discomfited by pictures of women from the southern Mursi tribe, who wear lip plates made of pottery. I also began to hear stories that the Mursi's pastoralist way of life was under threat because of intrusive visits by foreign tourists. The Mursi live in an area known as the Lower Omo Valley in south-west Ethiopia – a hot, lowlands region containing a number of exotic tribal people completely different to the highland peoples of Ethiopia.

Around 200,000 people live in this area, which was declared a World Heritage site in 1980. One of the other tribes living in the valley is the Hamer, whose striking women adorn their hair with red ochre pigment, and whose men hold demanding annual contests jumping over bulls. Another tribe is the Bodi, whose young men fatten themselves up every year so they can take part in a body fat contest. Relations between these various tribes in this region have not always been smooth, with a number of people killed over the years in disputes over cattle raiding.

In addition to the impact of tourism, these tribes are also dealing with huge changes in the way their grazing lands are being used. The Ethiopian government have been building a massive dam, known as Gibe III, in the Omo valley, primarily to boost the generation of electricity. The construction, which has attracted some international criticism on environmental grounds, entails moving some local people from their traditional territories. In the last few years the government has also been leasing massive tracts of land to agribusinesses from other countries, keen to grow crops such as sugar, cotton and palm oil on a vast industrial scale.

In early 2011 I was offered the chance to take part in a film project in this rapidly changing area, so I naturally grabbed it. The project was the brain child of a couple of hard-working and imaginative Masters students from Holland, Ilja Kok and Willem Timmers. They wanted to make a film about the uneasy relationship between the Mursi and the growing hordes of international tourists who invade their lands, travelling in 4x4s and armed with hi-tech cameras.

After an animated debate, it was agreed to focus the film on just two female characters – a Dutch tourist and a Mursi woman, complete with her lip plate. Willem and Ilja had already filmed a potential candidate in Holland and she was due to take a tourist trip soon in the Lower Omo Valley. However, they had no-one lined up yet from the Mursi.

Fortunately, the two intrepid students wanted to film at a time when I was in Ethiopia, so I gladly said I would go with them on location for some of the filming. Willem and Ilja went on ahead and a few days later, the cameraman Yidnekachew Shumete, a German journalist Carola Frentzen, and I made our way south for the shoot. We flew from Addis in a small Ethiopian Airlines plane to the enchanting town of Arba Minch, or Forty Springs.

Here we had a drink on the top of a cliff overlooking two beautiful lakes, Chamo and Abaya. The lakes are separated by a small neck of land, which forms part of a wildlife park called Nech Sar, or White Grass. Down below on the shore of Lake Chamo, dozens of crocodiles and hippos basked side by side in the sun. On a previous visit, my son Tim and I had taken a small boat out onto the lake to see these incredible creatures at close quarters. It all got a bit too close for comfort when the captain of our craft cut the outboard motor to enable us to drift ever closer and watch the hippos and crocs less obtrusively. Half-jokingly, my son and I said our goodbyes to each other. We were much relieved when eventually the engine was restarted and we returned to shore after our close encounters of the wrong kind.

On the next stage of our filming trip to the land of the Mursi, we travelled by jeep. Soon we were winding through the hills around Konso, famed for its circular, ancient terracing as a way of preventing soil erosion. I knew a little about this agricultural tactic, as one of my students had made a film a year before about a modern gang of workers still creating these terraces. Their day began with much blowing of horns to rouse everyone. The villagers then jigged and danced their way to work, singing merrily at every stage. After a few hours digging, it was time to repair to the Chief's house for some alcoholic sustenance and yet more dancing. I could think of many worse ways of living one's life.

After Konso we came to the town of Jinka, the gateway to the Mursi lands. The main dirt road used to double up as a makeshift runway for regular Ethiopian Airlines flights; these had been halted by the time of our visit, but while we were in Jinka, we did witness a charter plane coming in to land. I have never seen such basic air traffic control procedure. It involved a man waving a stick to keep the growing crowd of onlookers away from what had now become a landing strip. Although the plane was small, it churned up masses of dust and made a deafening noise.

In a sign of the times, the plane had been hired by a Dutch television team TV production team producing a reality show. This programme involved a Dutch and a Bodi family going to live in each other's homes. The Dutch family had just spent a few weeks with the Bodi, and now it was the turn of the Bodi family to be whisked off to Addis Ababa and then to Holland, mired in the depths of winter. It was hard not to feel sorry for the scantily-clothed Bodi family as they prepared to enter a totally unfamiliar and disturbing world – a fast-paced Western urban life amid sub-zero temperatures.

In Jinka we stayed initially at the German-funded South Omo Museum and Research Centre, perched on a hill overlooking the town. Several academics have based themselves here while conducting studies of the Mursi and other Lower Omo tribes. One famous observer of the Mursi was the Englishman David Turton, the first westerner to live among the Mursi for any significant period of time.

Ilja and Willem gave us a number of warnings about what to expect when we reached the Mursi village. They said it would be incredibly hot and dusty, with many annoying flies. In addition, the Mursi had a habit of noisily clearing their throats. Ilja and Willem had spent a number of nights in the village, sleeping in the chief's hut amid an army of mice. Our plan was to stay in tents right in the middle of the villagers' grass huts. I was already beginning to feel nervous about it. On the positive side, Ilja's and Willem's research had gone well and they had identified a strong Mursi woman called Nadonge, the wife of the number two chieftain.

Nadonge showing off one of her lip-plates

The drive to our Mursi village took about two hours, and involved bumping and scraping along a dirt track. We had to go through an inspection point where armed government security rangers were based to keep an eye on the Mursi. Our chosen village had been strategically established right next to the road to ensure the inhabitants could be easily seen by the international tourists. The Mursi are nomadic to some extent, but the lure of tourist gold is already affecting their decisions about where to set up camp.

There were about twenty huts in our village and we were immediately made welcome by Nadonge, who was one of the most influential characters in the settlement. It was hard to tell how old she was, but she appeared to be a strong woman in her early thirties. Although she was not wearing a lip plate when we first met, her mouth clearly showed signs that she did on occasion. Her bottom lip had been cut and it dangled freely several centimetres below her chin in a semi-circular arc. Mursi women have their lips cut in this way while in their teens; it's not totally clear why they wear these plates, which are fitted into those drooping lower lips. One theory is that it was a way of making Mursi women unattractive to the men of marauding neighbouring tribes.

The Mursi children were fascinated by our visit and quickly came over to where we were establishing our camp, right between several grass huts. We were offered some refreshment – a lump of what looked like dry maize and a green vegetable, which could have been cabbage but turned out to be something else. I was not keen at all on trying this, especially after being told that the maize concoction had been made with nearby untreated river water. However, I knew that, as an honoured guest, I had to show my gratitude, so I reluctantly pushed some of the unappetising looking food into my mouth. It was unpleasant, very dry and the cabbage-looking substance was extremely bitter. I managed to wash a few mouthfuls of this forlorn snack down with some life-saving bottled mineral water we had brought along with us. Already the water had reached a very warm temperature in the heat and humidity. It was like drinking from the hot tap. Nevertheless, I had done my duty – and managed to mutter some excuse after a couple of minutes of delicate chewing to avoid finishing the rest of the food.

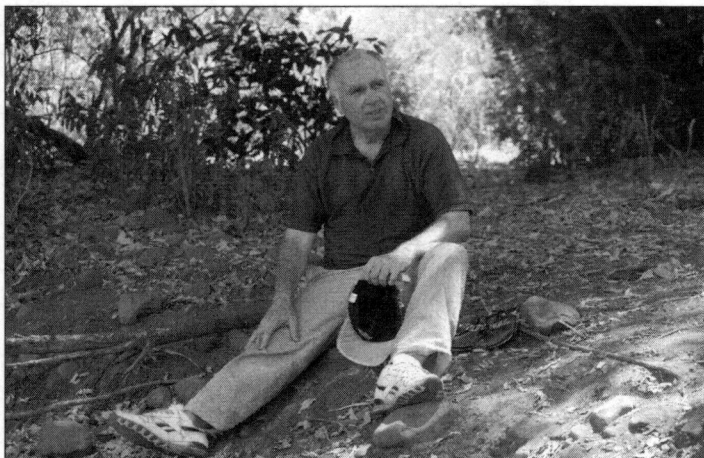

Taking a breather in the heat of the day

Although the women and children were relatively friendly, the men kept their distance. Some of them had rifles and other automatic weapons – all very disconcerting when you are stranded in the middle of nowhere. However, the men became friendlier when we shared with them some pasta we had cooked. We had a local guide and translator and he made it easier for us to settle in. The next day we were able to see exactly how the female villagers spent their days, including grinding a maize-like substance with two stones, and also fetching water from the river about about half a mile away. It was a beautiful walk there, with rolling hills in the distance. The temperature was so high in the middle of the day that we paddled in the river and lay in the shade under a tree as if we were lions on the savannah. Fortunately, there were no crocodiles in this part of the river or so we were told – the only threat to our peace and quiet was the attention-seeking of the Mursi children. They incessantly wanted to teach us some of the Mursi language and go through all our belongings. All I could manage was 'achale', an all purpose word meaning, among other things, hello, thank you or how are you.

Our main task, of course, was to do some filming, and we managed to catch some strong images from the village life. We also did an interview with Nadonge as she prepared herself for the visit of tourists, who normally turned up in the mid-to-late morning for an hour or so. Nadonge turned out to have a rapier-like wit and a developed sense of irony. She told us how she was puzzled why tourists wanted to take so many photos of the Mursi and she wondered what they did with all the images. She also described how they charged at least two birr for each photo, around 8p. The Mursi had become skilled in encouraging the tourists to take many photographs. They also charged two birr extra per person if there was more than one person in the photo. Nadonge told us they had had rows with tourists over interpreting these conditions. The Mursi even asked for extra payment if the feet of babies carried on their mothers' backs appeared in shot.

We filmed Nadonge daubing her face with lines of white paint made of clay to enhance her appearance for the tourists. She also placed cattle horns on her head – something the Mursi never used to do, but they have learned that the tourists consider this to be a more

Smile, you're on camera.
On photo duty with Mursi children and Ilja Kok.

authentic look. The lip plates were, of course, the centre
of attention and Nadonge had a range of plates that she
would wear and even sell. In normal village life she would
hardly ever wear a lip plate but, for the tourists, she would
insert specially painted plates into her dangling lower lip
for added affect.

For the Mursi, the tourist run had become big business.
The whole village whipped itself up into a frenzy before the
arrival of the foreigners. Babies were decorated in paint and
the young children tried to outdo each other by dressing
themselves in attractive, brightly coloured rustic clothing.

We also filmed with Nell, the Dutch female tourist
chosen by Ilja and Willem, as her group prepared to arrive
at Nadonge's village for what turned out to be a grotesque
orgy of camera clicking. The tourists wanted authenticity
but what they got was a warped commercial market and

This is how Nadonge looks most of the time, without her lip plate

Nadonge in full tourist battle dress

a complete clash of cultures. The Mursi were merciless in demanding their money for each photo. They harassed the tourists, who became alarmed and demoralised by the process. I could not blame the Mursi, though; they treated the whole encounter as a mere business opportunity and several of them would occasionally grin conspiratorially at us while they went about their morning's work. In a sense, both sides were exploiting and corrupting the other. It certainly left a bad taste in my mouth, even worse than the previous day's snack of the bitter green vegetable.

Close encounters. The Dutch tourist, Nell,
meets Nadonge in all her finery

Afterwards, Nell went through different emotions at having seen such a different culture. They ranged from joy to absolute disgust at herself and the Mursi for participating in such a cheap and demeaning encounter. Nadonge herself remained calm and aimed some barbed criticism at how stingy the tourists were. She knew that, to a westerner, 8p was absolutely nothing. She ridiculed many of the visitors who had hung on to their money in an attempt to drive an even harder bargain.

The Mursi seemed to treat us differently, as we were prepared to live among them, though of course we had to offer a facility fee to Nadonge for her time. I suppose you could argue that we were also part of the corrupting process, even though I felt our motives were more pure. Maybe the Mursi were just having a crash course into the benefits and drawbacks of free market capitalism.

Willem Timmers (left) and Yidnekachew Shumete sign up some new recruits

Because we stayed on site, we did witness some unique cultural moments. The most spectacular incident occurred when Carola and I were walking back from the river to the village. Suddenly, round the corner, we saw a group of tall Mursi men decked out like warriors with war paint on their faces and armed with spears. They were trotting along, moving menacingly and with terrifying purpose. It was hard not to panic. Somehow I tried to keep a bit of composure. I whispered to Carola not to look any of the marauders in the eye and just quietly move out of their path. I hoped they would ignore us but a couple of them stopped and awkwardly shook Carola by the hand. Fortunately for us, the whole group then quickly carried on its way.

Later, our guide told us what lay behind this terrifying demonstration of power: they were a group of elders sent out to find and punish a 21-year-old boy. He had got himself drunk and so had shamed himself and the tribe. The warriors were looking for him to beat him and teach him a lesson. And it was not only him – this war party was intent on finding all boys of the same age to also punish them as a sign that the rule of law was not to be messed with. I suppose you could call it an attempt to instil corporate responsibility.

Perhaps an even bigger challenge to the Mursi way of life than tourism is coming in the form of agricultural development. While we were staying in the region, the late Ethiopian Prime Minister Meles Zenawi was making a visit to the area to discuss the impact of the new dam and modern agribusinesses. We heard the drone of his helicopter overhead, already an unmistakable sign that the modern world was rapidly encroaching on the Mursi and other tribes in the Lower Omo Valley.

Such issues of development have dominated many societies since the Industrial Revolution transformed European countries in the 18th and 19th Centuries. Whatever the rights and wrongs, it is clear that these tribes in Ethiopia are the latest in a long line of civilisations which have been radically altered by the relentless march of economic and social development.

CHAPTER FOURTEEN

Epilogue

It is said that the economic future will belong to the BRIC countries – Brazil, Russia, India and China, though maybe it is a little soon to start writing off the United States. My experiences in Brazil and Russia have already been described earlier in this book. I have mentioned a little about China's activities in Africa but have not really said anything about India. It is a country I know something about, as I have been on a number of occasions in the last thirty years. Ever since meeting Mrs Gandhi way back in 1981, I have always had a thing about the country and find it to be the most fascinating, complex and different nation I have ever been to.

My first visit in 1982 involved a working tour of Bangalore in the south and Delhi in the north, where I was intoxicated by the country's ancient rhythms and chaotic infrastructure. My last visit in December 2012 was to watch England's cricket team in a match against India in Kolkata. Over this timespan, I have certainly seen big changes occurring in Delhi as it has turned into an increasingly modern city with its plethora of unleaded petrol rickshaws and new chic apartment blocks.

It is all too easy to be side-tracked by the widespread poverty and undeveloped rural areas in India. I remember when my eyes were first opened to the possibility that India was turning into an economic giant. In the mid-nineties, I had to go to Delhi to negotiate filming permission for a two-part series on the 50th anniversary of Indian independence, fronted by David Dimbleby. My local fixer was the indefatigable Sneh Gupta, a former actress who had a small part in the Bond movie *Octopussy*.

One evening Sneh took me to a party hosted by young professional people. It was a real sanctuary from the hustle and bustle outside and was packed with many impressive characters. One of them took great delight in predicting how powerful India would become. He pointed out that India's middle class was already around 300 million strong, about the size of the EU at the time. That, of course, was a massive market for companies selling apartments, fridges, cars and holidays. It blew my mind as I thought about the economic consequences of having such a big and burgeoning market right on one's doorstep.

The economic forecast I received that night has proved to be on the mark: India's economy has been growing at staggering rates this century and it is now flexing its muscles as part of the G20. There is obviously more growth and transformation to come – watch this space.

As for China, I only broke my duck in late 2011 when I went on a private visit to see what all the fuss is about. I had previously had some exposure to the Chinese way of doing business, as I had visited Hong Kong in the early nineties before it was handed back to the government in Beijing in

1997. In 2010 I also spent two months working for one of Bob Geldof's companies, Ten Alps Asia, in Singapore. It was all too easy to see the Singaporean Chinese community's appetite for hard work and an obsession with developing business acumen, but nothing had prepared me for China itself.

The scale of development is something to behold. As I travelled on the ultra-modern bullet train from Beijing to Shanghai, countless modern cities flashed by. Everywhere were new gleaming office blocks and huge flyovers on a bewildering array of modern motorways. According to a McKinsey Global Institute report, China will have more than 20 cities of more than five million people by 2025. The IMF says that by 2016, the America Age will end and the Chinese economy will overtake the US economy in real terms. Talk about a shift in the global economic and ideological tectonic plates!

I have a friend in his early sixties who once told me he would be glad he would be dead by the time, in his view, China takes over the world. But up close, Communist China does not seem as scary as when viewed from afar. On my trip I felt totally relaxed as a foreigner walking around and exploring. There was a lot to admire, including the Chinese can-do philosophy and its celebration of a cultural and spiritual past with many parks and heritage sites. I also glimpsed some of the more worrying aspects of modern China; when I met the producer of a Western television organisation based in Beijing, she told me about the widespread surveillance of the population by secret police and the incredible pressures placed on those who dare to speak out with a different vision to that of the state.

It was hard though to get a sense of what ordinary Chinese make of their country's rapid economic advancement and how that is impacting on their psyche. I did, though, manage to gain an intriguing insight about modern social attitudes prevailing in the country at the time. While I was in Beijing, the Chinese were undergoing a serious bout of soul-searching following a hit and run accident involving a two-year-old girl called Yueyue. The accident in a busy market in the southern town of Fusan in Guangdong province was publicised by the social network site Weibo, the Chinese equivalent of Twitter.

What was so shocking to Chinese sensibilities was that, after the girl was hit twice by two vehicles, she was left bleeding in the road without anyone going to her aid for several minutes. According to agency reports, more than a dozen people passed by and simply ignored her. It was all captured on closed circuit television. Eventually, a female street cleaner helped her and called in her mother. Yueyue died a week later in hospital from her serious brain injuries.

When these distressing images were spread by Weibo, there was widespread questioning about whether there was now a moral vacuum in China and whether the country was changing for the worse, despite – or perhaps because of – the galloping economic progress. Were the seemingly uncaring passers-by merely heartless or were they frightened by the possible repercussions of publicly taking responsibility to help Yueyue?

It is all too tempting to rush to easy conclusions about China's dizzying economic advancement and believe that the world is about to change dramatically forever. No-one really knows whether the Chinese economy can keep performing at such an intense level for decades to come without coming apart at the seams. However, what is clear is that we in the West will have to share many of the current resources we enjoy with the emerging middle classes in the East. This will be a significant shift as Western living standards are put under increasing pressure. It is ironic that I began my career at the BBC with the Soviet brand of communism failing and yet, thirty years on, it is Western capitalism that is under threat and creaking alarmingly.

This competition between the pure market forces philosophy of the West and authoritarian capitalism of the East will undoubtedly lead to more widespread global changes. It is not the only show in town, of course, as the world also has to grapple with a multitude of other issues such as dwindling energy resources, rising populations and environmental stresses.

As we look ahead, it is intriguing to think about how such future events will be covered in the news media, and how we will evaluate them for ourselves. In the electronic age we don't even have to leave our houses any more to view images from pressure points around the world. We can access many places and events via our computers, and can easily unearth written or visual material from eye witnesses involved in stories from even the remotest of areas.

There are many benefits of being able to track down first hand sources rather than having everything mediated through a travelling correspondent. The information age can create tremendous freedom and opportunities to think for oneself, and I greatly welcome most of what is happening.

However, it is not too fanciful to think that the age of the traditional foreign correspondent may be coming to an end. We have to embrace change, of course, but I believe we may well miss something by not having independent-minded observers going to a particular place and being able to pass on insights from a more detached perspective. The danger is that reasoned observation and reflection may be drowned out in a partisan and perplexing world.

Over my lifetime, I have usually found that seeing something for myself leads to more understanding than being a consumer of information from afar, when you can be at the mercy of pushy, vested interests. My recent trip to China is a case in point. There is no substitute for getting your own feel and smell of a place. You can learn a lot by surfing the internet, but there is nothing like being in the thick of it. I therefore hope that the tradition of foreign affairs reportage, as displayed in this book, will continue.

Throughout my career, I am glad to have had so many chances to go and see for myself – and pass on whatever understanding I have gained to others. In our uncertain world, the law of impermanence will always be in force. All things must change, in world affairs and in our own lives. There will be plenty of history left for all of us to view.